'I have been privileged to have known Josh and the family for many years; dipping in and out of their lives as a fellow autie. Josh explains very clearly and concisely what it means to live on the autism spectrum. His many stories of life encounters take the reader on an unforgettable journey connecting them with the reality of life on the spectrum. This book not only illustrates one life with Asperger syndrome but paints the backdrop to so many others. In doing so it helps to equip its readers with knowledge and the know-how to enable them to walk beside us. Those who read this book will find countless ways to support us and our families, appropriately preventing the circumstances that lead to bullying and mental health distress. Well done Josh…an unforgettable read!'

– Dr Wendy Lawson, psychologist, qualified counsellor, social worker, autism advocate and author

'Written in an easy, conversational style, this fascinating book is both an illuminating autobiography and a wise and extremely useful insider's guide to growing up with Asperger syndrome. Comprehensive and detailed, the book is packed full of perceptive insights and practical strategies that can support individuals with AS – through school, college and beyond. Revealing a deep understanding of his own 'special interest', Josh writes with disarming honesty, sharing some intensely difficult experiences as well as many happier ones. He gives us a positive message, a practical reference, a sense of hope – and an appreciation of the many special qualities of individuals on the autism spectrum.'

– Jude Welton, author of Can I tell you about Asperger Syndrome?

D0376409

'Every parent and indeed everyone who works or lives with children or young people with autism should read this lovely book. No one better understands the condition than someone who actually has a diagnosis and lives with it. In this book Josh manages to link professional theories to his own personal development and gifts us with what he has learnt along the way. In my 30 years of working in the world of autism I have not read a more valuable book and throughout it Josh's humour shines through. It is good to read a book that not only explains the way a person with autism sees the world and the challenges to be faced but also highlights the strengths people with autism have that can, with the right encouragement, enable them to understand themselves.'

– Jane Vaughan, Director of Education, The National Autistic Society

'Joshua's book is a highly readable book that covers many of the challenges of life on the autistic spectrum from childhood to early adulthood. Drawing extensively from modern research, and also from his own experience, it manages to be more than just a reference text. Joshua articulates with precision how his disability has impacted on his life. His evaluation of sensory difficulties superbly addresses an area which can be overlooked when considering the needs of a person with autism. I suggest that many young people may also wish to read the book, as it contains a Toolbox specifically designed to overcome the many challenges life presents. This is a young man who deserves our attention.'

– Anna Kennedy, autism campaigner

RAISING MARTIANS
FROM CRASH-LANDING
TO LEAVING HOME

of related interest

The Complete Guide to Asperger's Syndrome
Tony Attwood
ISBN 978 1 84310 495 7 (hardback)
ISBN 978 1 84310 669 2 (paperback)

Freaks, Geeks and Asperger Syndrome
A User Guide to Adolescence
Luke Jackson
Foreword by Tony Attwood
ISBN 978 1 84310 098 0

The Passionate Mind
How People with Autism Learn
Wendy Lawson
Foreword by Rita Jordan
Illustrated by Lisa Simone
ISBN 978 1 84905 121 7

Parenting a Child with Asperger Syndrome
200 Tips and Strategies
Brenda Boyd
ISBN 978 1 84310 137 6

RAISING MARTIANS

FROM CRASH-LANDING
TO LEAVING HOME

HOW TO HELP A CHILD WITH ASPERGER
SYNDROME OR HIGH-FUNCTIONING AUTISM

JOSHUA MUGGLETON

FOREWORD BY TONY ATTWOOD, PHD

Jessica Kingsley *Publishers*
London and Philadelphia

First published in 2012
by Jessica Kingsley Publishers
116 Pentonville Road
London N1 9JB, UK
and
400 Market Street, Suite 400
Philadelphia, PA 19106, USA

www.jkp.com

Library of Congress Cataloging in Publication Data
Muggleton, Joshua.
  Raising martians-from crash-landing to leaving home : how to help a child
with Asperger's syndrome or high-functioning autism / Joshua Muggleton.
      p. cm.
  Includes index.
  ISBN 978-1-84905-002-9 (alk. paper)
  1. Asperger's syndrome in children. 2. Parents of autistic children. I. Title.
  RJ506.A9M84 2012
  618.92'858832--dc23
                                2011027923

British Library Cataloguing in Publication Data
A CIP catalogue record for this book is available from the British Library

ISBN 978 184905 002 9
eISBN 978 0 85700 523 6

Printed and bound in the United States.

To John and Julia, my parents
They picked me up when I fell down
They pushed me when I needed to run
They let me soar when I needed to fly

DISCLAIMER

In this book, I talk about my experiences: these experiences are true, and any similarity to anyone else's is purely coincidental. I have done my best to put very complex facts in a simple and easily accessible way. This may mean that some more complex facts and theories are missed out. This is a basic practical introduction. All the advice I give in this book is based on my experiences and the experiences of others and what we have found has worked. This does not mean that the same solution will work for everyone. However, I hope I will have given you enough information on the problem for you to formulate your own solution.

CONTENTS

FOREWORD

Tony Attwood

Joshua is the friend that every child with Asperger syndrome (AS) seeks and needs. He is also the person parents and teachers want to listen to in order to understand AS, and want to eagerly ask questions of for his sage advice. Although Joshua is only in his early twenties and was not diagnosed as having Aspergers until he was 15, he writes with remarkable maturity, honesty and engaging passion from his personal experiences. He is also an eloquent communicator and a student of Psychology, so his explanations and advice are based on personal, scientific and clinical knowledge. This combination provides a unique insight into how someone who perceives themselves as a 'Martian marooned on planet Earth', tries to relate to life on an alien planet.

Joshua is a prospective clinical psychologist, and while some may be surprised that a person who has AS could be a successful psychologist, it is important to remember that an intelligent and constructive survival strategy for someone with AS is to study people in order to acquire the ability to relate successfully to them. Joshua explains that his interest in psychology helps him to predict people's behaviour. He has spent over two decades observing and analysing people and has become a translator of the Asperger way of perceiving, thinking and relating to neurotypicals. His voice is that of the child who has AS in your home or in your class, and he has important messages to convey.

The book enables the reader to explore the main characteristics of AS and how these specific abilities and differences affect the person's life at home and at school. Joshua recognises how experiences, and especially the attitudes of peers, can affect mental health and contribute to clinical depression. Chapter 3 on sensory sensitivity provides an explanation of the sensory world as perceived by someone who has AS. Parents and teachers often fail to recognize how aversive some sensory experiences can be for a child or adolescent who has AS. Chapter 4 on repetitive behaviours and interests is enhanced by Joshua's personal explanation of why he engages in behaviours that are annoying to others. He describes how these behaviours are successful coping mechanisms for people who have AS, who often have considerable difficulty explaining why they engage in specific behaviours. Joshua provides a clear, coherent and logical explanation, using personal insight that is substantiated by scientific studies and clinical experience. His writing style is engaging and he has a remarkable ability to use metaphor to explain a concept or strategy. Reading Chapter 5 on friendships, I particularly enjoyed his description of someone with AS not needing as many friends, or seeing them as frequently as peers, as being similar to a 'social camel'.

Acquiring daily living skills, such as being independent in self-care skills, budgeting and using transport can be difficult to achieve for someone who has AS, especially during adolescence and the young adult years. This can be crucial to achieving the ability to successfully leave home. Joshua provides good advice that is important for parents to read, whatever the age of their son or daughter. He also provides wise advice for teachers in creating an Asperger-friendly environment at school. The child often feels an alien on another planet and needs guidance and understanding from peers and teachers. Bullying and teasing reinforces a feeling of alienation and Joshua's description of when being different is not cool is accurate and harrowing to read.

When you have read this book from cover to cover, you will know what it feels like to be a Martian who has crash-landed on Earth, but you will also appreciate how heroic those people who have AS are, living in a world that has so many social zealots, who at times appear to be illogical and intolerant of anyone who is different. You will also have feelings of hope and optimism, as well as many new ideas to help you enjoy a Martian in your home and classroom.

Tony Attwood, PhD
Minds and Hearts Clinic
Brisbane, Australia

ACKNOWLEDGEMENTS

At this point, tradition states the author thanks people who helped them make the book who they didn't have the money to pay off. However, this book wouldn't have been possible if it wasn't for the people who got me here. Thank you all.

First, my mum. When I first wrote this book, each chapter was a long monologue, based on what I talk about in my lectures and workshops. She spent many months going through my pages of thoughts, ideas and musings to make them flow in an easily readable manner. She also brought some of her personal experience and parental perspectives into the book, which I hope has made this even more readable for parents. I am indebted to her for her time, energy and persistence. I also need to thank my dad, who encouraged me to start talking to groups about Asperger syndrome in the first place, and to write the book. He also played a large part in organising the content of the book. Both have been a huge help in so many ways with the book. Not only did they bring me through incredibly hard times, but also they have helped me to get to where I am today. A son could not wish for better parents.

I have known Melanie Carr for seven years. In that time she has been a big sister to me, a translator of the obscurities of social life, and even an adviser on this book. She has kept me going through my darkest moments – and even made me laugh. But most of all she has been my friend.

Lea-ann and Andy from Farleigh. They took me, a broken shell of a person, with little hope left, and helped make me whole. Without them, A levels, university, and life beyond would be just a dream.

Hatty and Phil, my academic parents. They took a nervous, out-of-place fresher and settled me in at university. They got me out of my shell and involved in life. They showed me how to enjoy myself at university. For this I am forever grateful.

Last, but not least, I would like to thank Stacey Martin for the excellent cover design. She rarely shows off her artwork in public, and so I am very grateful for her allowing me to twist her arm into doing it.

INTRODUCTION

Who am I?

Since the age of 15 I have been invited to give talks to parents, teachers and other professionals about how they can help children and young people with Asperger syndrome in their care. After nearly every talk, I have been asked if I have written a book they could buy. I suppose I have just got tired of saying no.

This book is designed primarily for parents, teachers and others who work with people who have Asperger syndrome. I will start from the very basics, but that said, even old hands will find this book useful, as unlike most books, I won't just be spouting theory at you. I will also take you through *why* something is a problem and try to get you to see life though our eyes. I will give you the solutions to problems that I have found work for me and *why* they work. Everyone is different, so what works for me, may not work for you. But I hope that after reading this, you will be equipped with the knowledge to make your own solutions. Think of this as the insider's guide to Asperger syndrome, something that gives you all the facts but in plain English and in a form you can use.

So who am I? What qualifies me to write such a book? Let me tell you my life story.

• THE GOOD YEARS

I was born in Guildford, England. My father, John, was a computer programmer at the time, working mainly with programming and testing payroll software. My mother, Julia, was an ex-music teacher, and can to this day play more instruments than anyone I know. I was a normal baby. There certainly wasn't anything unusual about me.

My earliest memory is of being at playgroup. They had a toy windmill. I found it fascinating. The relationship between the rate you turn the handle and the rate the blades spin. The way the blades appeared to go faster at the end of the spin than at the beginning, and the way they kept spinning even if you didn't turn the handle. I spent a lot of time looking at that windmill. However, I didn't spend a lot of time actually playing on it. Because it was everyone's favourite, there were always other children using it, and I just didn't want to spend my time with them. If I shared it with them, then I wouldn't be able to turn the handle at the speed I wanted. I wouldn't be able to try and work out the fascinating relationship between the speed of the handle and the speed of the blades. The other children wanted to play games, pretending that sand was flour, which seemed to me a strange thing to do. Why should I bring sand to one end, only for it to be swept to the other end and put into another bucket? It served no purpose. Of course, the staff would try and get me to join in. However, I quickly realised that if I cooperated for a few minutes they would stop watching me, and then I could go back and stand staring at the windmill.

Mum thought it would be good to home school me for the first few years. This was great for me, as I didn't have to do much socialising. There was a home school group which we attended, but for the most part I was having fun counting cars and making graphs with Mum, and then sitting down to watch *Number Time* on TV.

But it wasn't to last. About a year later my younger brother Jack was diagnosed with autism. He had very little speech and didn't really respond to people, although he always seemed quite happy in his own little world. My parents had suspected autism for some time but it was still a shock to have it confirmed. They were desperate to try and help him, to reach into his world and for him to reach into theirs. So they decided to try to work with him one-to-one in a fairly focused way, with volunteers helping. Because of this they decided it would be best for me to join a mainstream school.

THE BAD YEARS

My parents were worried that I might have trouble adjusting to the new environment and making new friends, so they arranged for me to spend a few months just going in for a half day, and then working up to a full week. The school also arranged for me to have a 'buddy' who could draw me into his social group, but this didn't happen. I was a poor runner; my legs would flail wildly and if I was lucky I would get some sort of forward motion. Because of this, kids being kids, they always chose me to be the chaser in chasing games. I would spend my time desperately trying to catch them, while they teased me. This didn't help my self-esteem. The other favourite playground game among the boys was football, and I was equally hopeless at that. They soon decided I was beneath their consideration, and I was left to hang around on my own, feeling awkward. I felt very alone and helpless.

I started eating more chocolate, a *lot* more chocolate. It was the only thing that made me feel happy. I also started wearing more clothes. This was partly to conceal the fact that I was putting on weight, and partly because it made me feel safer. Have you ever been to an interview, and felt really warm, but you don't want to take off your jacket or jumper, etc.? Do you feel like doing so would somehow expose you, or make you more vulnerable? That is what I felt. We sometimes use clothes as a barrier, as protection, and so in class, I would always wear a jumper. Even if it was a hot summer day and other people were sweating profusely, I would keep my jumper on. When it was break time, I would add my coat to this. This was a very thick winter anorak, and I would wear it zipped right up with the hood over my head, walking along the different coloured lines on the playground. The coat may have made me feel a bit light-headed with the heat, but it also made me feel safe. I didn't notice the others and I hoped they didn't notice me.

I went through several years of this, and by the end of my time at primary school I felt very low. My slightly odd behaviour had raised some eyebrows, and I did meet with a clinical psychologist, who basically told me it was my fault, and to be normal. Needless to say, that was not helpful, and made me much more resistant to help later on in life. However, I did see a glimmer of hope. I thought secondary school would be much better. I thought people would be nice to me. I was looking forward to studying more subjects, and I was even wondering what GCSEs I would take. My only worry was that I would get a detention. I found the idea of getting a detention shameful, and also quite scary. A detention was a mark that I had done something wrong, and worst of all, I had to get my parents to sign to say they had seen that I had a detention – the shame. I would rather die than get a detention. But, I reasoned with myself, detentions must be only for kids who misbehaved, and I definitely wouldn't misbehave. So it would be okay.

The week I started secondary school, someone in my class got a detention, not for any bad behaviour but for simply forgetting to bring the right book – something that is easy to do if you study ten or more different subjects. This terrified me. We each had a locker where we could keep our books and physical education (PE) kit, but whenever I tried to use it I was pushed and shoved by other kids, because the lockers were all crammed in together. Because of this, I decided the best thing to do would be to carry every book and every bit of kit around with me every day. My bag weighed over four stone, and my first one quickly broke under the weight. To this day I still stoop slightly because I spent day after day carrying an extremely heavy bag around. I was anxious all the time, sure that I would inadvertently break a rule or forget the homework or not hand the homework in to the correct place at the correct time. The huge bag I carried on my back and my panic-stricken face made me an easy target for other kids, and I soon came to fear them too. By the end of that first month I was depressed, and by the end of the term I was feeling overwhelmed and suicidal.

It became very important to me to keep home and school separate. I think I felt that the only place I could relax and let my guard down was at home. So I would try to do all my homework at school, working through break and lunch times in the library. I was too stressed to eat, so there was no point in trying to have a lunch, and break times were difficult, so I preferred to avoid them. If I didn't complete all the homework during school, I would do it as soon as I got home, making sure I had finished it all. Only then would I change out of my uniform, have something to eat and drink, and try to relax. This was difficult because I knew the next day would be just as hard.

I was under so much stress, that my recollections of the next four years are patchy. Some memories are burned into my head, because they are so traumatic, and even now I just don't think about them. Others are fuzzy at best. But what I do remember is that every day seemed to get worse. I was the weird kid who had no friends, so people would trip me up in corridors, kick my chair, try to make me say silly things, or just deliberately wind me up. They made sure that even the library wasn't safe for me. I would report this to the teachers, but after a few months even they just ignored me.

I want to make it clear right now that I do not in any way blame my teachers. They had had no training so they did not know how to recognise Asperger syndrome, let alone how to help. Often when they tried to help, senior management would make it impossible. It didn't make any difference that I went to one of the top state schools in the south-east of England. I didn't receive any appropriate help and support.

I also started seeing a clinical psychologist and psychiatrist, initially for my depression, but they soon realised there was something else going on. At age 15, they finally diagnosed me with Asperger syndrome. This did not come as a shock to me. I had self-diagnosed myself at age nine, after listening to a lecture by Dr Tony Attwood at the University of Surrey (I was a very geeky child!). However, I hoped that with a diagnosis would come understanding from the school. This did not happen.

JUST WHEN THINGS COULDN'T GET WORSE...

Eventually, when I was 14, one day I cracked and had a complete nervous breakdown. Usually, I would be able to fight off the panic that would envelop me every day on waking, or at least control it enough to get into school and cope with the day as best I could. But one day Mum drove me to school as usual, and I simply couldn't let myself get out of the car. The assembled hordes of Genghis Khan could not have got me out of that car. The same happened for the next few days. I would come home and spend the day shivering under a blanket, curled up in the foetal position and in a state of complete nervous exhaustion. It became clear to everyone that I had finally been broken.

At this point, EOTAS (Education Other Than At Schools) came along, to try and get me back into school. Initially, they would just drive me up to the school gates, and home again, then into the building, then for one lesson. For a few weeks, I would make progress. Then I would collapse again and have to start from scratch. They also suggested to the school that it might be prudent for me to drop subjects like French (of which I could not speak a word), Art (which I simply didn't get) and PE (where I was a laughing stock). The school's response was along the lines of 'Of course, why didn't you say so earlier?' which was particularly infuriating, since for the past few years my parents had been begging them to let me drop PE, only to be met with 'We cannot change the curriculum.'

However, it wasn't enough. Eventually, in my GCSE year, my psychiatrist signed me off school as I could no longer cope and the struggle was doing long-term damage to me. I tried very hard to study as I didn't want to flunk my exams. I had eight hours of private tuition a week, but it was like trying to make up for almost five years of lost knowledge. I could hardly remember anything I had been taught in school, because I had always been too anxious to take it in properly. When the time came to take the exams I couldn't face the idea of actually going back in to school to sit them, so an alternative venue was arranged (the council offices). After a note from my psychiatrist of extenuating circumstances, I managed to scrape seven grade Cs and a B.

REBUILDING MY LIFE

The next year, I needed to recover: I was terrified of leaving the house, and I felt very fragile. I was still keen to learn, so I did self-study with Satellite Virtual Schools, an internet-based study programme. I started doing AS level Computing, Physics, Economics and Maths, although my teachers had to go back and fill in some big gaps in my knowledge of GCSE material. Every week I was sent work to do, which I would complete and send back, via the internet, to be marked. This worked well for a few months, but when it came to my exams, the pressure got to me again, and I had to stop working.

After taking over eight months off, I started at a specialist residential college near Bath. Farleigh Further Education College is specifically for people with an autistic spectrum disorder (ASD), mostly people with Asperger syndrome. The students all went to various mainstream colleges during the day for tuition (I went to City of Bath College), which was supported one-to-one with a key worker from Farleigh. Back at base, Farleigh provided support and guidance. Moving away from home was a huge step that I would not have normally taken. I had spent much of the last year hardly venturing out of the house. The first few months were really hard. After I got my A levels, Dad told me the story of how he had kept a full tank of fuel in his car, as he was expecting a call saying I couldn't cope with it. But I knew this was the only way forward, and that kept me there. The specialist college worked for me because they gave me one-to-one support whenever I needed it. Often it would just be someone sitting behind me during the lessons making extra notes for me. Because the person who worked with me (the wonderful Lea-ann) had time to get to know me, she knew when I was getting stressed, and she also knew how to help me.

I believe that my experience shows how, with a little bit of the right support, we can flourish. The support I got wasn't rocket science: what helped were simple, common-sense things that could be done in any school. People with an ASD shouldn't need to move a hundred miles from home, as I did, to get the help they need, and only the lucky few are able to go to specialist colleges as not many of these colleges exist. The placement cost the council over £75,000 a year, but all I really needed was someone to support me in lessons. This could have been done at home, for a third of the cost.

For the first year, I studied Maths, Business Studies and Physics. After a poor result in Physics, I dropped it in favour of Psychology. I found I really enjoyed this subject, and if anything the pace was too slow. I decided to do the whole A level in one year so that I would finish all the subjects in two years. I soon realised that I could have enough points to go to university – something that I had not even thought about since secondary school, when my grades started to fall. I quickly applied to a range of universities to study my new found passion, psychology. I applied to St Andrews on the off chance that my grades ended up better than expected. However, after taking a trip up and falling in love with the small Scottish town, I knew I had to go there. I started obsessively checking UCAS (Universities and Colleges Admissions Service) to find out if the notoriously competitive St Andrews would offer me a place. They did, and that summer I managed to achieve a very strong A in Psychology, a good A in Maths, and a B in Business Studies – enough to meet their offer. The moment when I found I had achieved the necessary grades to take up this offer must count as one of the best in my life.

I was very nervous about going to St Andrews, not least because I was coming off antidepressants, and had a documentary film crew watching me. However, before I got my results, I got a call from Student Support Services. Since I had mentioned my Asperger syndrome on my university application, they thought it best to get in touch, and see what they could do to make the transition as smooth as possible. I am really grateful to Malcolm, my student support adviser, who went out of his way to make St Andrews a safe place for me.

I was also lucky enough to get my academic mum before I even started university. Academic parenting is an excellent student-run tradition at St Andrews, where two third or fourth year students (a mum and a dad) adopt freshers. This dates back to when students would come to university at a young age, and would still need a mother and father figure. Dad (my real dad) happened to mention to a family friend I was going to St Andrews. She had a daughter, Hatty, in her final year there, and mentioned it to her, who in turn offered to adopt me. I still remember her waiting at my hall to welcome me, and help me move in. She went through the freshers' schedule with me, and helped me prepare, as well as introducing me to my future academic dad, Phil, and the 'Ents Crew' (Entertainments Crew), through which I made many friends. I met often with my academic parents, and that simple support they gave me was probably the most valuable.

At this time, I also found out I was to be followed for a year by a documentary film crew for the Channel 4 series *Year Dot*. The support I got from the thousands of people who contacted me online, supporting and encouraging me, was really heart-warming. I also became good friends with the film crew themselves, who were always really encouraging.

I am now in my final year at St Andrews, and I am not looking forward to leaving. People say leaving St Andrews is one of the hardest things you have to do. I have my own academic kids now, making me feel very old. I have responsibilities with the Ents Crew, which I enjoy doing. I am also a regular Bop DJ – something I would never have done before, if it was not for the Ents Crew and my friends encouraging me to try it. I have so many friends here, so many memories, it feels like home.

MY 'AUTISM CAREER'

I have two younger brothers who have both been diagnosed with autism. Since my diagnosis in 2004 I have been giving talks to teachers, parents and professionals. I was asked to help launch the National Autistic Society's 'Make School Make Sense' Campaign in the House of Commons to over 200 Members of Parliament (MPs), peers and celebrities. I wrote a blog for two years for the same campaign. I have also spoken on the BBC and CNN, and as I mentioned, I've been followed by Channel 4's *Year Dot* programme. I am also lucky enough to be the youngest ever councillor for the National Autistic Society (NAS). It is my ambition in life to become a clinical psychologist. I want to help others overcome their difficulties and realise that, if they try, and if they have the right help, they can succeed.

I love public speaking. For me, it is easier than talking to somebody one-to-one. If I am talking to a crowd of a hundred people, or to a TV camera, I am not having a conversation with another person, I am talking at something. In a one-to-one conversation I have to keep track of a lot of things: making eye contact, reading body language and understanding the subtext of what is being said. When I am giving talks, I don't have to take all this into consideration. I believe in the importance of explaining, expressing and communicating the way people with an ASD experience the world. I hope that my talks give some guidance as to what changes will work. I don't want other people to go through the bad experiences that I had. Education is the key. If people can understand Asperger syndrome and autism, then we are beginning to build a world where we can flourish and make our own contribution.

1

ASPERGER SYNDROME

Welcome to Mars!

'What would happen if the autism gene was eliminated from the gene pool? You would have a bunch of people standing around in a cave, chatting and socialising and not getting anything done.' (Temple Grandin, a woman with autism, Associate Professor of Animal Science at Colorado State University, speaking at a conference on autism in 1998, quoted by Baron-Cohen 2002)

Let's briefly look at how autism and Asperger syndrome were first discovered.

EARLY CASES OF AUTISM

Autism has probably been around for most of human history, if not all of it. In her book, *Autism: Explaining the Enigma*, Uta Frith (2003) talks about some historical case studies which describe people who would now be termed autistic. However, it is only in the past 50 years that the particular pattern of difficulties (and strengths) that we now know as autism has begun to be recognised.

Hans Asperger and Leo Kanner

The first person to realise that there might be a distinct subgroup of children among those with severe learning difficulties was Leo Kanner. Kanner was an Austrian psychiatrist working in the United States from the 1920s up until his death in 1981. He saw that a lot of children being referred to his clinic exhibited the same sort of behaviour. He described them as having a lack of awareness of other people, often treating them like they weren't there, or as objects. They had an amazingly strong desire for routines, which were often hugely complex and elaborate. He also noted problems in communication; either an unusual style of communication, or none at all. He published his findings in 1943. Initially, few people took an interest in his work, but as time went on, more professionals recognised this characteristic profile of abilities and disabilities among the children they worked with.

At the same time, in Europe, another Austrian psychiatrist called Hans Asperger was looking at an unusual group of people. He was working mostly with children and adolescents who were much more able and, like Kanner, he noticed a subgroup who had a distinctive pattern of difficulties and strengths. He described them as having problems making social contact with others. Their social approaches were often inappropriate, out of context, and generally naive. They seemed to have very good grammatical skills, and often had a very comprehensive vocabulary, and yet when they talked, it was as if they were talking at you, rather than with you. He saw they frequently had a very strong interest in certain self-directed subjects, such as timetables. They were often very capable academically in some specific areas, yet found great difficulties in others. My favourite observation is that he observed a 'marked lack of common sense', a trait I think is sometimes ignored. Asperger, like Kanner, thought the condition was present from birth, but that it often didn't become evident until the child was over three. Asperger published his findings in 1944, but it was not until the 1970s that his work became known outside Western Europe. When Asperger became aware of Kanner's work, he acknowledged the similarities between the two groups of children studied, but also maintained there were distinct differences.

Lorna Wing

By the 1980s autism was generally recognised, but until the 1980s, Asperger syndrome was largely unknown. Lorna Wing changed all that. In 1981 she published her groundbreaking book

Asperger Syndrome: A Clinical Account. This served to bring to light the work of Hans Asperger, and make people take note. The term Asperger syndrome started to be used, and finally, the research that had been done since Asperger and Kanner was all starting to fall into place.

PRESENT DAY CASES

Nowadays, autism and Asperger syndrome are estimated to affect about 1 per cent of the population. If we apply this statistic worldwide then there are 60 million cases of autistic spectrum disorders all over the world. You would have thought this would mean everyone would know about it. However, people's knowledge of ASDs is often very clouded. Many people think of the 1988 film *Rain Man*, which portrays autism as the ability to count cards, to be a whizz with numbers, a general genius. While I won't deny that this is a good film, many people now think of this as a typical case of autism. This is not true. Of all the people with Asperger syndrome and autism that I know (which is a lot!) I can only think of one person who even comes close to the abilities shown in the film, and even he cannot count matches in a second or remember whole telephone directories. I'm not denying that there are some people with autism who do have an exceptional ability, but this is relatively rare. The individual the film is based on, Kim Peek, was not only autistic, but also a savant. Savantism is a very rare condition, where someone has areas of brilliance, and also areas of disability. While people with ASDs have areas of expertise, these are rarely at a level that would be classed as savantism.

Unfortunately, Asperger syndrome has also been in the media for the wrong reasons. The unfortunate case of Gary McKinnon, the hacker diagnosed with Asperger syndrome who is currently fighting against extradition to the United States, is a sad example of where Asperger syndrome and the law can conflict. Conversely, one or two people with Aspergers have been wrongly accused of committing crime simply because they are loners, and may not articulate enough to explain themselves. In reality many people with Aspergers get very anxious about committing the most minor infraction of rules, let alone breaking laws. For example, when I was at school there was a one-way system for walking along busy corridors, and I would never walk even one metre the wrong way because it would be breaking the rules. Even when my classroom door was just two metres into the one-way system, and it would save me a three minute walk, I would not break that rule. Often when offences are committed, it is due to one of two reasons. We either do not understand that what we are doing is wrong, or we are under extreme stress.

FAMOUS ASPIES

As a contrast to this, I think it is always encouraging to look back at historical figures who may have had Asperger syndrome (AS) and have made outstanding contributions to their field, perhaps because of their Asperger ability to focus and pursue a train of thought long after everyone else has given up. I must stress that there is no proof that these people had AS, but it's fun to speculate.

Albert Einstein

Arguably the most famous name in science, Einstein revolutionised physics with his theories of relativity, and his famous equation $E=mc^2$. But what about his childhood? He didn't speak until he was three, and when he did begin to speak, he repeated the same sentences over and over again, until he began to speak normally at the age of seven. His teachers reported that he was a poor student. As an adult he was a very confusing lecturer. Whether this was due to him or to his subject, I don't know. Some people say that because he spoke out on political issues, and had several intimate friends and several affairs, that this would rule out Asperger syndrome. However political views, having friendships, and having a love life are all perfectly possible with Asperger syndrome.

Isaac Newton

Newton is another great scientist who may have had Asperger syndrome. It is reported that he was a very quiet individual who rarely spoke. When he became very engrossed in his work, he would go without eating. He was notoriously bad tempered with everyone around him. When giving lectures, if nobody turned up, he would continue to give them, talking to a deserted room. When he was 50 he had a nervous breakdown, due to his paranoia and depression, but this doesn't detract from the outstanding contributions he made in the fields of science and astronomy.

Other historical figures

Einstein and Newton may be perfect examples of people with Asperger syndrome who found their niche in life, and because of that, managed to excel. Other amazing historical figures who may have had Asperger syndrome, including Lewis Carroll, Beethoven, and Mozart, are discussed in Michael Fitzgerald's (2005) book, *The Genesis of Artistic Creativity: Asperger's Syndrome and the Arts.*

SO WHAT EXACTLY IS ASPERGER SYNDROME?

In a nutshell, all autistic spectrum disorders (both autism and Asperger syndrome) are affected by the triad of impairments. The 'triad of impairments' is a phrase first coined by Judith Gould and Lorna Wing during a research project in the late 1970s (Wing and Gould 1979). It is used to describe the three main areas of difficulty, which are communication, social interaction and imagination. Roughly this means:

- The way we communicate verbally with other people.

- How well we get on with other people.

- To what extent we are able to imagine what the other person might be thinking and feeling in a particular situation. Imagination also includes the ability to generally think flexibly.

In reality it's difficult to separate these areas as all three are aspects of social interaction.

With Asperger syndrome the triad of impairments often results in the following:

- Pedantic speech, or a very literal understanding of words (for example, being confused by expressions such as 'get a move on').

- A lack of understanding of the social rules.

- Frustration at communication problems, and at being different.

- Very focused thinking rather than flexible thinking. The advantage of this is that we often become experts on a subject that interests us. The disadvantage is that we find it difficult to deal with disruptions in our routines.

However, Aspergers is a very varied condition, and can present in many different ways. I discuss this in more detail later in this chapter.

THE AUTISTIC SPECTRUM

The autistic spectrum is right at the core of autism and Asperger syndrome. The problem is that Asperger syndrome and autism are so varied in the ways they present themselves in individuals. There are lots of behaviours that could be described as 'autistic' but each behaviour on its own doesn't mean much. Take something like knowing every fact about a subject. A lawyer has to know so many laws and presidents – does that make them autistic? Do they have Asperger syndrome? Nope. What about social ineptitude? I think we all know someone who is always quiet at parties, keeps themselves to themselves, occasionally makes social gaffes. Does this single fact qualify them for a diagnosis of Asperger syndrome? No. This is where the autistic spectrum comes in.

The idea is that the more autistic behaviours you have, and the more severe they are, the further along the autistic spectrum you will be. At zero, there would be people who are extremely social and are great communicators. These people would be extremely neurotypical. Neurotypical is a term used to describe someone who is 'normal', someone who does not have Asperger syndrome or autism – your average Joe on the street. As we move along the spectrum, we begin to get people with one or two 'autistic traits'. Perhaps they have some social difficulties, or pedantic speech, or a need for routine and sameness. Someone who shows autistic traits in more areas of their life, or who shows autistic traits more strongly, would be further along the spectrum. These would be the people with Asperger syndrome. The more strongly the person shows autistic traits, and the more their everyday lives are limited by this, the further they would be along the spectrum. These people would be described as autistic. Eventually, at 100, there would be the people who have no speech and who only respond to other people in a fairly limited way. These people are severely autistic. This is the autistic spectrum – but remember the numbers are just illustrative; in reality it is often much harder to pinpoint where on the spectrum a particular person might be.

PLACING PEOPLE ON THE AUTISTIC SPECTRUM

So what is the distinctive pattern of traits that would indicate an autistic spectrum disorder? Psychologists tend to look for evidence that the person is affected by each of the elements of the triad of impairments, that is, communication, social interaction and imagination. In reality it can be difficult to judge. Some people obviously have Asperger syndrome as they clearly display the characteristic difficulties. Other people may show one element of the triad more than the others, or may show evidence of the triad of impairments in a subtle way. Also, it's possible for an individual to change. Some people show their Asperger tendencies much more when they are stressed. If they are in a good environment, it may be hard to detect their 'aspieness'. It is possible for someone to learn ways around their autistic traits, or they may become better at disguising them. So it is possible to move along the spectrum in either direction, at least to a certain extent. That said, you cannot 'cure' or 'grow out of' autism or Asperger syndrome, only adapt. I tend to think of it like a bungee cord, attaching us to our specific spot. For example, I can hide my Asperger syndrome reasonably well, but when I get stressed I am pulled back to my point on the spectrum (or temporarily a little further sometimes).

Rather confusingly, we tend to refer to someone with Asperger syndrome or autism as being 'on the spectrum', and disregard neurotypicals. For example, I might say the people on the spectrum make up 1 per cent of the population. Actually this is not factually true, as the spectrum *includes* neurotypicals, so technically, 100 per cent of people are on the spectrum. From now on, unless I say otherwise, when I refer to people on the spectrum, I am talking about people on the spectrum who are not neurotypical.

THE TRIAD OF IMPAIRMENTS

As we have seen, the three elements of the triad of impairments are communication, social interaction and imagination.

Communication

We tend to think that words are the most important part of communication. But when we have a conversation words constitute only 9 per cent of the information we give and receive about feelings and attitudes; the rest is from nonverbal cues, like body language or tone of voice (Mehrabian 1981). Our body language, eyes and tone of voice speak volumes. You can tell when someone is bored or agitated or annoyed by the way they are sitting. You know from their gestures when they are being firm and definite, or when they are unsure, or when they are becoming more relaxed. Their tone of voice, the speed at which they are speaking, the hesitations, the rise and fall in pitch, all add to the picture. Their facial expressions, the moments when they look at us sharply or turn their eyes away, or when they gaze at us and smile, give us a greater awareness of what they are trying to express. All of this works together to increase your understanding of what they are saying. Because much of this is lost on people like me who have Asperger syndrome, we find it much harder to communicate with the richness you do.

Whether you are aware of it or not, you automatically take account of all of this extra information that body language gives. When someone uses just a simple phrase like 'I'm fine,' you know whether they are really fine. You know if they are just saying that to sound okay, but are actually upset or annoyed. You would know if they are saying 'I'm fine' in a sarcastic way. We are not so lucky. We have to really think hard in order to pick up on these subtleties. For us it is a conscious effort, and a very tiring and demanding one at that!

Think of the background music in a film. The music amplifies the mood of a scene. It gives you the feeling that something scary is about to happen, or makes you well up with tears when something very sad happens. It can echo the emotional nuances of the drama as it unfolds. To an extent it can make you feel what the people in the film are feeling, so that you understand the story better. Now imagine the same film without any background music. It would be less engaging. It would be harder to work out what the people in the film are feeling. You would need to concentrate more to work out the meaning of what was happening in the film. Body language is a bit like the background music in a film; it conveys a lot without us even realising it. For people with Asperger syndrome there is no 'background music' of body language. We don't understand body language so we miss out on a whole layer of meaning.

One aspect of body language that deserves special attention is eye contact. Many people with AS find this particularly difficult. Try staring into the eyes of someone you don't know particularly well for longer than you should; it quickly begins to feel very uncomfortable. That's how I feel with normal eye contact; it's like trying to stare at the sun. The result is that we are even less likely to notice facial expressions and pick up the meaning the expression might convey. Other people with AS don't make much eye contact because they are unable to get much information from the facial expressions of other people, so there is no reason to make eye contact. The problem with a lack of eye contact is that the other person can think you are not listening or that you are not seeing their point of view. I find it helps to look at the middle of the other person's forehead, just above the eyes. That way the person I'm conversing with thinks I'm making eye contact. It's worth noting that some people with an ASD make too much eye contact. They fix the other person with an unwavering gaze while they go into a monologue about their favourite subject. Eye contact is one of those tricky social behaviours that it's hard to get right.

In everyday life there are dozens of different social cues to pick up on. For example, the cues that let you know when someone wants to finish a conversation or the cues that tell you it is your turn to speak. Our problems with reading these kind of cues mean that we sometimes unintentionally butt in, or we make the opposite mistake of not taking our turn, which can be frustrating when we have things we need to say. The verbal ping-pong of a conversation is quite difficult for us to get right, and the problems multiply when we are in a group situation.

Given the complexities of face-to-face conversation it's understandable that a lot of us prefer communicating via email. That way we know exactly what the other person is saying and have time to think about the best way to reply.

Unfortunately words themselves can also be confusing to people with Asperger syndrome because we tend to take them literally. For example, when my youngest brother, Jordan, was younger he started playing board games. He was told to throw the dice, so he threw them across the room. This was not because he was trying to be clever but because he was following the instruction in a literal way. It's surprising how much verbal information can be confusing if taken literally. For example, 'pay attention' (how does this involve money?), 'hold on', meaning wait (what am I meant to hold on to?), 'fed up' (eating a lot as a metaphor for being miserable?) and 'keep in touch', which means stay in contact, not keep touching. Common figures of speech such as 'he was over the moon' or 'he was gutted' just seem bizarre.

But if we sometimes have a problem with the phrases most people use, you also have a problem with the way we speak. We sometimes tend to talk *at* people rather than talking *to* them or *with* them. There are a number of reasons for this. First, it's hard to read facial expressions and to work out what they mean. So we can't easily tell from facial expressions if the other person is getting bored or impatient. This makes it hard to know when to stop talking. Second, we also enjoy talking a lot about our favourite subjects and tend to assume other people will find it equally enjoyable listening. A lot of social chit-chat seems a bit pointless to us, so we feel more comfortable talking about something we know about.

Third, another problem with our speech is that we can sometimes be too pedantic. I think this is particularly evident when an aspie gets on to his favourite subject and uses all sorts of technical words that the other person may be unfamiliar with. This can seem like showing off but it's more often because the person with AS doesn't realise he needs to adjust what he says depending on the knowledge of the person listening. This is something most people do without having to think about it. Sometimes we use words which are precise but are not in common use, such as 'therefore' or 'evidently'. My family tell me I use the word 'thus' sometimes in my talks, thus sounding a bit pretentious (still, it is better than when I said 'sort of' and it started to sound like 'sod off').

Finally, some people with AS, as Hans Asperger himself observed, tend to use a flat, monotonous voice when they speak. They leave no pauses between their words so they can make quite sure they can say everything they want to say without interruptions. As much as we have problems reading nonverbal communication, we can also have problems giving it. We can seem fine but, in reality, be feeling really anxious – as is often the case at school. Therefore, it is important to remember that just because someone with AS or autism looks fine, it doesn't mean they are.

Social interaction

You could say it's a myth that all people with Asperger syndrome prefer to be alone and don't want a social life. In reality there are some aspies who are happiest when they are alone doing whatever interests them. These aspies are only minimally interested in socialising. There are other aspies who spend a lot of time alone, not because they want to, but because they are painfully aware of their social shortcomings. They would rather be alone than risk awkward social encounters. A lot of aspies do socialise but know they are somehow at a disadvantage. This produces anxiety because they are not quite sure what they should be doing or saying. It also causes frustration because they are often not able to put their views across effectively. Still other aspies don't consider that they have any problem socialising, but other people think that they do. These aspies tend to be tactless, or they interrupt, or perhaps they talk at length about their favourite subject but are not particularly interested in what the other person has to say. This annoys other people but the aspie is oblivious to their reaction. Finally, there are aspies who are actually quite extroverted but make lots of social gaffes without being aware of it. Often people find their naivety and their trusting nature endearing, but it does make them quite vulnerable to being tricked or exploited.

What varies is:

- the individual's desire to socialise

- their ability to sense whether a social interaction has been successful

- their feelings if the interaction has not gone well.

One person with AS may only be making minor social errors, but may be very aware of them and feel quite bad about it. He worries that he has upset or annoyed the other person, or that he has made himself look foolish. This type (my type) cannot easily tell whether the insult is something which people will think 'Oh, he must have meant xyz,' or whether we have deeply insulted or offended them and started a family feud. Another person with AS might make lots of errors but be quite unaware that he has annoyed other people. Yet another person with AS may realise an interaction has gone badly but will not be particularly concerned about it, having said what he wanted to say. So the same deficit can present in different ways, depending on the individual's personality and their level of awareness.

What we all have in common is a deficit in social understanding. Essentially this means we are not good at 'reading' other people. We have difficulty in picking up the moment-by-moment social cues which signal what's going on in a conversation (which links to the communication impairment). But also, at a deeper level, we find it hard to work out what the other person might want or feel or believe in a given situation. This links to the impairment in imagination, because to work out what the other person might be thinking or feeling we need to use our imagination to understand things from their perspective.

An important part of social interaction is the ability to make sense of other people's behaviour. This involves recognising how another person might be feeling and why they might be feeling that way. For example, if I see someone with a cross facial expression who is speaking very emphatically, I have learned that he is annoyed. If this person is a teacher who is talking to some pupils, it's fairly obvious for you that the children have broken a rule and that is why the teacher is angry. You notice the feeling a person seems to be displaying, and we notice what's happening that might have caused that reaction. People with Asperger syndrome vary in their ability to make sense of behaviour in this way. Many situations involve behaviour and emotions that are much more complex. Anger, distress and joy are emotions that are easy to recognise. Irritation, embarrassment, suspicion, anxiety and scorn are more difficult to recognise and are caused by more complicated thought processes. We aspies might not realise that the person we are talking to is becoming irritated or anxious. If we do realise it may be unclear to us why they are responding in that way.

An impairment in this area matters because it sometimes makes it difficult to understand what is going on. As an adult it's hard to deal with people effectively if you are not good at 'reading' their reactions. The other person can feel annoyed or hurt if you don't respond in the right way. They may not understand that you genuinely don't realise how they feel. In a conversation a neurotypical person can monitor the other person's reactions and may change the way they are saying something to get a better response. We aspies sometimes lack this sensitivity and flexibility.

My youngest brother Jordan has a diagnosis of autism. He often doesn't fully understand social situations, particularly if he is in a more complex situation such as a group. He finds it difficult to 'read' one person, so keeping track of what is going on in a group, making sense of everyone's behaviour, is quite hard. It's a problem when he wants to get the group to play his choice of game; other people always seem to have more say in who does what, which is quite frustrating for him. Jordan would love to be popular but has no idea how to achieve this. For example, if any of the other children in his class are misbehaving, Jordan will tell the teacher. This is because he believes that they shouldn't be breaking the rules. He even tells the other children to stop being naughty because it might upset the teacher. It's very hard to explain to him why being good in this way is not likely to make him popular. He isn't able to imagine how a child who is being naughty might feel when Jordan warns the teacher.

Another problem Jordan has is in understanding that it's possible for someone to say something that isn't actually true. Some of his friends at school claim their parents allow them to watch a fairly notorious cartoon which has a 15 certificate. I think it's quite unlikely that they are really allowed to watch this programme, and it seems obvious they are just boasting. But Jordan is sure it must be true because 'they said so'. He can't imagine why his friends would say something if it isn't actually true.

Although people with Asperger syndrome have difficulties with social interaction, this can eventually become a source of strength. People with AS can become original and independent thinkers. This is because they have to rely on their own judgements. They don't automatically do the same things as everyone else and think the same way as everyone else. They are less influenced by their social circle because they tend to be less involved with a social circle. This leaves them free to pursue their own ideas.

Imagination

As we saw in the previous section, imagination plays an important part in social interaction. To an extent we have to imagine what the other person is thinking and feeling in order to make sense of their behaviour. But an imagination is also important in other ways.

An impairment in imagination is not an inability to imagine anything, but is a tendency to think in an inflexible way. The minds of many neurotypicals tend to be a bit like a search engine on the computer. Take one word, for example 'lemon', and you can come up with hundreds of associations. This would include not only facts to do with lemons and citrus fruits, but also mental images, memories, recipes, colour schemes, even scents. Neurotypicals are very good at thinking in this flexible way. In contrast people with AS tend to think in a very logical way. We are very good on facts and details and are often very systematic and thorough, so if you ask us to think of the word 'lemon', we will more often think of *the word* lemon.

This ability to think imaginatively and make lots of connections affects everyday life. It makes you more able to anticipate what will happen and therefore prepare yourself mentally. For example, suppose a class of ten-year-olds are told that their usual teacher is ill, so they will have a supply teacher instead. Neurotypical children will probably remember previous years they have been taught be different teachers. They may chat to each other about what the supply teacher might be like. They may remember a story or TV programme which featured a supply teacher. By remembering relevant experiences and sharing information together they gain a better idea of what having a supply teacher could involve.

Children with Asperger syndrome are less likely to be able to do this. They will have had other teachers in the past, but as these were not specifically 'supply' teachers, they may not realise that those experiences might be relevant. They may have had a supply teacher in the past and therefore assume that must be the person coming to teach them because that was *the* supply teacher. AS children are probably less likely to chat to other children about what's going to happen. They may not realise that a supply teacher is only temporary. Neurotypicals can draw on lots of memories and experiences, and share information with other people, in order to get a better idea of what is going to happen. Their flexible thinking enables them to generalise. Aspies are less able to make connections and realise what could be relevant.

Although AS thinking is less flexible than that of neurotypicals, this is not always a disadvantage. We tend to be very thorough and focused in our study of a subject, which can sometimes give us an advantage in subjects like Maths, the Sciences and Engineering. We like to work out causes and effects, to find the rule and the exceptions to the rule, to find the rule which governs the exceptions, and to make lists of all the examples. We are very focused and can follow a train of thought for a long time. We can spot little inaccuracies and are often perfectionists. We also tend to be very thorough.

My brother Jack, who has autism, is fascinated by people's heights. He spends hours researching heights on the internet. He has produced a list of the heights of hundreds of celebrities, starting at 5 foot 10 and working downwards in quarter inches. He studies predictive height charts and makes graphs of the average height distribution of 18-year-olds in the UK. He knows the average height of both males and females in different countries. Yet he has a problem crossing the road because it requires flexible thinking. We can't just give him a simple rule such as 'If you see a car coming, don't cross' because then he will not cross even if the car approaching is a long way away. By the time that car has finally passed there may be another car on the horizon that he would wait for. Crossing the road requires flexible thinking which adjusts quickly. Obviously most adults with AS don't have a problem crossing the road, but Jack highlights the strengths and weaknesses of autistic thinking.

Another aspect of inflexible thinking is the need to be able to predict what's going to happen. We are less able to adjust flexibly to the unexpected. When you can predict something you feel safe, don't you? You would probably feel disconcerted if something you took for granted suddenly changed. For example, if the government suddenly decided that, starting today, we should always drive on the right side of the road instead of the left, you would probably feel confused and quite annoyed. It would be difficult to adjust to this radical change. People with AS find much more minor changes unsettling. If my train gets delayed, or if a lecture room is changed, or if my routine is disrupted in any way, it can cause me some anxiety.

Children with AS often seem particularly unsettled by the unexpected. For example, one boy got very angry at a barbecue because he was served a burger in a bun but without chips. Other people may have thought his behaviour unreasonable – he was having a tantrum just because he wanted to have chips. But whenever he had had a burger before, it had always been served with chips, so he assumed that it was the rule that chips were an essential part of a burger meal. To him it was as outrageous as giving him just the bun with no burger in it. This doesn't excuse bad behaviour but it does make it more understandable.

Lots of upsets with AS children are caused by the predictable suddenly becoming unpredictable. For example, if the child's class 'always' goes swimming on a Tuesday and then one week they don't, or if the family usually takes one route to Granny's house but then one day they take a different route, an AS child can get very upset. It's as if taking a different route to Granny's could mean they weren't going to Granny's at all. Or if the swimming trip is cancelled one week, it might mean they would never go swimming again. They may not be able to think about what might happen instead of swimming, which can be even more stressful.

Inflexible thinking can also cause a problem with generalising from one context to another. I enjoy cooking but I find that knowing how to cook in one kitchen is very different from knowing how to cook in another. The recipe is the same but everything else is different, and this difference seems to unsettle me more than most. This problem with generalisation can sometimes affect the way a child with AS learns. Jordan knows that $2\times9=18$. However, if he is told, 'Two boys each have nine apples. How many apples are there all together?', he won't necessarily understand that the two times table is relevant.

An important aspect of the impairment in imagination is a tendency to have restricted and repetitive patterns in interests, activities and behaviours. In fact this is specifically mentioned in the diagnostic criteria for an autistic spectrum disorder, along with the triad of impairments. The way this tends to manifest in people with Asperger syndrome is in a narrow focus of interest. This often actually becomes a strength. We like to study a particular subject until we know it and understand it completely. Sometimes the interest isn't an academic subject. For example, Jack is quite an expert on *The Simpsons*, and other people become fascinated by phone masts or types of vacuum cleaners. It can still become an absorbing hobby. Often the skills developed in its pursuit, such as researching on the internet and cataloguing data, are transferable. Jack taught himself to make graphs and understand averages in his studies of height. If you happen to find some fellow enthusiasts, it can lead to the development of friendships.

I think part of the reason for our passion to learn all about a particular subject is a need for control. For us the world often seems a very unpredictable place. If we know all there is to know about our pet subject, we feel there is at least one area of life we have mastered completely. Jack can predict exactly what will happen in any given episode of *The Simpsons*. I love psychology because the more I learn, the better I can predict people's behaviour. If your subject is bus timetables, you know when the bus will arrive and where it will go.

People with AS tend to stick with the familiar in their daily lives, for example always eating the same food for lunch or sticking strictly to a particular daily routine. Again, this is usually an attempt to gain control in some small way, and limit unnecessary variables. Suppose your best friend has just bought a new house which is really difficult to find. The first time you visit, you plan the route carefully and arrive on time. Suppose your friend then suggests a quicker route for next time. The chances are you might still stick to the route that's familiar because you are sure it works. It is the same for us, except on a much wider scale. If we find a way of doing things that works, we will keep doing it because it makes us feel safe and in control. For my university lectures, I tend to arrive early, and watch the other students come in. About 90 per cent of them go to the same seats day after day. Why? Because they feel comfortable there, they know who is likely to sit next to them, what the view is like, and in some cases, how loudly they can talk without the lecturer noticing. To an extent, everyone likes to stick with the familiar because that way we cut out unnecessary distractions and can give our mind fully to the task at hand.

So what does this all mean?

Let's put this triad of impairments into play in one of the simplest and most common situations anyone faces: watching TV. If you decided to go and watch TV, you would probably just go and sit down and watch. There would be no real effort in it. But it would be different for me. Ideally I would want to watch my choice of programme, maybe with subtitles, watching some sections twice, and that would be that. I wouldn't need to worry about what anyone else thought or felt.

In reality I have to consider things like a whole host of things. Who else is in the room? Are they already watching something? Do I want to watch it? How amenable might they be to me changing the channel? Are children in the room? If so, would my choice be suitable for children? Is someone just waiting for their favourite programme to come on? Is there a queue or rota or other schedule I should be following?

You might also take some of these things into account, but you seem to be able to do so without much conscious effort. You seem to be able to size up a situation, perhaps ask the other people in the room a couple of questions, and then know how to proceed. But when I walk into the room, I have to weigh up all the different factors in order to work out what I should do. And I can't just stand there for a few minutes thinking about it in case that looks odd. You don't need a mental list of questions because you seem to instinctively know what is and is not acceptable when you enter the room, but I don't. You can predict what will happen if you put the TV on really loud, or if you just change channels without asking. Sometimes I can't, even if I really think about it. I have to try to imagine what people will do, how they will react. Of course some people with AS have the opposite problem. They would just walk in and take over the TV and not really understand why other people get annoyed.

This scenario shows how the elements of the triad – imagination, communication and social interaction – are used by neurotypicals all the time in daily life, and how an impairment in these areas makes life more complicated:

- *Imagination* – knowing how people will react if you take a particular course of action.

- *Communication* – knowing what kind of question to ask, and knowing how to explain what we ourselves would like to do given the choice.

- *Social interaction* – knowing the way to ask the questions and the way to interpret the answers (does 'do what you like' mean 'do what you like' or does it mean the opposite?).

In some ways the three elements are all aspects of the same process, which could perhaps be defined as 'social imagination'.

WHAT IS THE DIFFERENCE BETWEEN AUTISM AND ASPERGER SYNDROME?

Tony Attwood, a leading mind on Asperger syndrome, has said that the difference between autism and Asperger syndrome is happiness (Attwood 2001). I think this is very true. Someone with autism may be very different from the general population but be quite unaware of it. Someone with Asperger syndrome is usually much more aware that he is different to everyone else, even though the differences are more subtle. And there is an expectation in society that we should be like everyone else and could be if we only tried a bit harder. This can be quite hard for people with Asperger syndrome. First, because we are out of place. It's like turning up for a gathering wearing jeans and a T-shirt, only to discover that everyone else is dressed in dinner jackets and bow ties. There is nothing wrong with jeans and a T-shirt. A T-shirt and jeans are very practical if you want to get things done, but everyone else is busy standing around socialising. Because of our culture, we tend to automatically think that if we are not normal we are wrong – abnormal or subnormal – when in fact we are just different. We have just as many strengths as everyone else. It just happens that our culture particularly values sociability. People with Asperger syndrome have the awareness to realise that their strengths are often not appreciated and valued, while their weaknesses are often highlighted.

Because we have this self-awareness, we often realise that if we try to act the same as everybody else then we are more accepted. This is certainly what happened to me. I knew I was different from quite an early age, and as soon as I started getting bullied for it, I adapted. I mimicked others and I tried to blend in and become like them. It was a case of interACTING rather than interacting. The person I projected still didn't get on very well with other people, and I was still bullied. But I think that I would have been bullied more if I hadn't worn that mask. I think this may be one of the reasons why I wasn't diagnosed with Asperger syndrome until I was 15. I seemed to be just like everyone else. Even my parents, who were familiar with autism because of Jack, dismissed the idea that I might have AS for a long time. They knew I was really struggling but didn't recognise the cause.

People with autism, on the other hand, tend not to develop this awareness that they are different from everyone else. If they do develop it, it usually worries them less. Society itself is more tolerant towards people who are obviously autistic, and it has to take steps to accommodate them. But people are quick to judge those of us who have more subtle difficulties.

In the end there is no clear-cut dividing point between autism and Asperger syndrome. Some people are obviously autistic, others obviously have AS, but many are somewhere in between the two.

VIEWS ON ASPERGER SYNDROME

As Asperger syndrome affects so many people, and in so many different ways, people are bound to have their own ideas and perspectives on its cause, and what should be done. I am only going to briefly touch on two major views.

Extreme male brain theory

The extreme male brain theory was put forward by Professor Simon Baron-Cohen at Cambridge University in 1999.

Let's think about men and women. Who do you think are better systemisers? Systemisers are people who are good at organising data in a logical way. They are able to understand technical and mechanical systems easily. Most people say men are better systemisers, and they would be right. It is one of the reasons we like do-it-yourself (DIY), or at least think we do until it gets too hard. What about empathisers? Who is better at chatting with people, making relationships, tuning in to how another person feels? It is quite obviously women. This is not to say that all women love socialising and hate DIY, or that every man is a geek or a grease monkey, just that, in general, men are better at systemising, and women are better at empathising.

Let's think about systemising again. It involves an orderly, logical, thorough way of thinking. It involves working out how things operate. Who else could be described in this way? Aspies generally like routine and order, and we are often very good at understanding technology. We much prefer dealing with logical facts to dealing with people. In fact, most aspies are systemisers who are just a bit stronger in their tendencies. Hence extreme male brain theory of Asperger syndrome.

In fact, extreme male brain theory is an extension of Baron-Cohen's original Empathising–Systematising (E–S) theory. A test is available online which provides you with your empathy quotient (EQ) and systemising quotient (SQ) (see http://eqsq.com). It's full of statements such as 'I really like going to parties' or 'If I had a collection of CDs, I would want to order them'. You have to decide how strongly you agree or disagree with each statement, and this gives you your score. A low EQ score and high SQ score indicates that you are a systemiser. If there is a sufficiently large discrepancy between the two scores it's quite likely that you have Asperger syndrome, or at least Asperger traits (see Baron-Cohen 2008).

Genetic cause

It does seem that autism and Asperger syndrome have a genetic component. Hans Asperger was the first to note this, in his original paper, where he saw that parents often had some similar behaviours. When I look at my extended family, I can see many Asperger traits. For example, there are a couple of mathematicians, and several who work with computers. They are clearly very good at the kind of logical, orderly thinking that is typical of people with AS. Most of them have a bit of aspieness in their personalities, though probably not enough for a diagnosis. Often when parents receive a diagnosis for their child and learn more about Asperger syndrome, they notice Asperger traits in other relatives, or in themselves. While genes are not the sole cause of Asperger syndrome, they clearly play a large part. Scientists have found at least one gene that seems to be related to autistic spectrum disorders. However, there are undoubtedly more genes involved, and many complex interactions going on, making this a very complex area of research. This research has also resulted in greater efforts to find a cure for autism and Asperger syndrome. It has also resulted in a growing eugenics agenda aimed at eradicating it.

A CURE FOR AUTISTIC SPECTRUM DISORDERS?

We now know a lot more about autistic brain chemistry and genetics so it's possible that in the future a cure will be found for some autistic spectrum disorders. Already there are people and organisations claiming to have found a cure by using medical, dietary or behavioural interventions. However, these have not been proven by independent research. Certainly there are some treatments that can *help* some people with autism or Asperger syndrome. However, I have met a few of these people who claim to have been cured, and I see someone who has learned to hide their Asperger syndrome or autism well. They have learned to adapt to their environment, but they still often show some social naivety, or other typically autistic traits.

But should society be looking for a cure? I know there were times when I was at secondary school that I wished there was a cure for what I had. But now I have got through that, I realise how valuable Aspergers can be. If you learn how to use it, it can be an advantage rather than a disadvantage. Far more worrying is a eugenics agenda and the possibility of forced treatment of Asperger syndrome and autism.

EUGENICS

The idea behind eugenics is that defective genes should be strained out of the population. There is a growing movement, particularly in the United States, of people who believe that once we have identified an autism or Aspergers gene, and can reliably screen for it, we should routinely screen and abort foetuses who carry this gene. In short, remove autistic spectrum disorders from the population. But many of the great minds in history may have had AS. If we eliminate Asperger syndrome from the gene pool then we will have no more Einsteins, no more Beethovens and no more Andy Warhols. Society needs people who see things in a different way, in order to grow and develop. Many of the most important discoveries in many different areas of knowledge have been made by people who had a different perspective to everyone else, and the single-mindedness to pursue that perspective.

Everyone has strengths and weaknesses, and has to learn how to build a meaningful life which makes the most of their strengths. We all have to learn how to work on our weaknesses, or to find ways of adapting to them. At university I see people who clearly have Asperger traits. It's our Asperger traits that help us focus on the task in hand, use our logical minds and not get distracted with socialising.

I have seen low functioning autism. I know a young girl of 17 who isn't verbal, and who has very little understanding of the surrounding world. I know how difficult it has been for her family. But they would be the first to point out that, given the right environment, she fully engages with life in her own way. In the wrong environment and without the right support, it is extremely difficult. But surely society can be judged by the humanity with which it treats its most vulnerable people? If we weed out the autistic spectrum gene, then in my opinion human progress is going to slow substantially.

WHY ARE THE RATES OF AUTISM AND ASPERGERS INCREASING?

Something odd is happening with the autistic community. It seems to be growing larger. Since the 1990s autistic spectrum disorders have become one of the most common neurological conditions affecting about 1 per cent of the population. Why is this happening? I think there are several reasons.

First, most professionals didn't know about Asperger syndrome until Lorna Wing published her book in 1981. Prior to that people with AS were just thought to be a bit eccentric and socially awkward. Now lots of research is being done so professionals are far more aware and far more knowledgeable. Also the concept of the autistic spectrum with its triad of impairments has resulted in the more subtle manifestations of autism being recognised, whereas previously only very obvious cases of autism were diagnosed. For example, when Jack was a toddler the paediatrician declared that he couldn't possibly be autistic because he had just made eye contact with her, and because his behaviour was not wild.

Second, there is greater public awareness, so people are more likely to seek a diagnosis, particularly if they are experiencing difficulties. Often help is available only if there is professional recognition that there is a problem. A diagnosis doesn't guarantee help but it can be a step towards accessing much needed services. This, too, contrasts with the situation years ago, when there was little educational provision available that was autism-specific, and a diagnosis of autism was more likely to close doors than open them.

Third, I think it is that society is changing. In the past the rules for socialising were more formalised and provided a person learned the rules and stuck to them, they could manage reasonably well. Now society is much more fluid and the rules are far more subtle, so it's possible to move quickly up or down in social estimation depending on how socially adept you are. And often a person has to follow different rules in different contexts. For example, teenagers need to behave one way with their peer group, another way with teachers or employers, and yet another way with their family. This makes it harder for people with AS to remain undetected.

Finally, I think that the presence of autism and Asperger syndrome is growing simply because more people are being born with it. In my opinion, a liking for systemising, an ability to focus in a single-minded way, and an independence of thought are all attributes that people with Aspergers bring to society. While I think it is a bit farfetched to claim we are the future evolution of man, it seems reasonable that having a good number of us can be useful to the human race.

2

MENTAL HEALTH

Where Normal isn't a Setting on a Washing Machine

What exactly is good mental health? Most, if not all of us, are a bit peculiar, whether it is an obsession for football, an addiction to a specific TV show, or simply an enjoyment of cleaning! When it comes to mental health, we are all different, so perhaps everyone is abnormal. As someone once said, 'normal is just a setting on a washing machine', and that is probably the best way to look at mental health.

Having said that, there are some conditions associated with Asperger syndrome that can have a significant impact on our quality of life. In this chapter I cover three aspects of mental health that sometimes occur with AS – depression, meltdowns and anxiety. I will also look at strategies on how to help people who have these conditions.

DEPRESSION

The word 'depression' seems a bit inadequate for the state of mind it describes. It seems to imply a listless apathy or feeling a bit 'under the weather', when actually it can often be a wretched experience full of anguish about the past and hopelessness about the future.

My depression

Talking about depression from a clinical and practical point of view won't give you an insight into what it is like to have it. This is why I am going to tell you a bit about my experience. My depression was caused in two ways, first, the never-ending bullying I received at school, and second, the lack of teachers' understanding. The bullying started at primary school, but got much worse when I moved to secondary school when I was 11 years old. Pupils would trip me up in corridors, tease me, and deliberately irritate me. The teachers also made things worse, not deliberately, but they simply didn't have the training to know how to help me.

Imagine being tortured; but instead of the pain being on the outside, it is inside you. It is not in your body, it's your mind. You try to scream out in pain, to beg for it to stop, and yet nothing comes out of your mouth. This is how it felt for me. After a few months of this when I was 12 or 13, I started saying in all seriousness that I wanted to die. I couldn't take it any more. My GP sent me to a psychiatrist, who prescribed some antidepressants, although they may as well have been mints for all the effect they had.

Before Christmas one year I tried to kill myself. I remember going into the bathroom with my school tie. I tied it around my neck and then pulled it to make it tighter. I just kept pulling, making it tighter and tighter. I felt the pressure building in my head, and my vision started to distort in time with my pulse, which I could hear loudly in my ears. Eventually I got too scared and loosened the tie. I realised that even if I had kept going, I would probably just have passed out. My grip would have weakened and the blood would have come back to my brain. When I look back, I think I just did it because it helped the pain to go away. The brain gets all worried about the lack of blood and forgets about school tomorrow. I continued to feel that low for the next four years, over which time I would try and kill myself at least two more times, possibly more. I don't remember clearly. I give this account not to scare you, but because you need to be aware of what can happen. That way you have some chance of stopping it.

How can you tell if someone is depressed?

Recognising depression in another person once it becomes established isn't too difficult. However, typically it begins very subtly. The person starts to realise that they do not get any pleasure from things that they used to enjoy. This quickly leads to a feeling that it's pointless to bother doing things that they were previously keen to do. Ordinary setbacks are interpreted as evidence of their own flaws and failings, and reasons are found to discount positive things ('it must have been an easy test', or 'they just said that to be nice'). The person starts to behave differently over several weeks. They become more withdrawn and/or angry, they don't seem to enjoy anything and they seem preoccupied with gloomy thoughts.

However, those of us with Asperger syndrome sometimes mask how we feel, either because we don't trust other people to respect our feelings or because we ourselves think we shouldn't be feeling this way and don't want to admit it to others. Equally, as you may recall from Chapter 1, not only are we bad at reading body language, but also we are bad at giving it off too. We also often have problems communicating those feelings verbally too. This may lead to the depression getting progressively worse until we finally crack and perhaps self-harm or even make suicide attempts. This means that parents, teachers and carers need to be vigilant to make sure that as soon as they suspect there is a problem, it is acted upon.

Here are some signs to look out for. These are by no means definitive, and if you suspect depression, do not fail to act simply because I do not list a symptom you see here. This is just based on my experience and, in part, the definitions in the DSM and ICD (*Diagnostic and Statistical Manual* and *International Classification of Diseases*, which are big medical books of different disorders and diseases: APA 2000; WHO 1992).

Change

Yes, I know 'change' is a very broad term, but a change in behaviour is often a sign, particularly in a person with AS, as we tend to stick to a routine more than most people. This could be a change in appetite (either overeating or a lack of appetite), a change in sleeping habits (sleeping more or less), or a change in the intensity or the focus of our latest obsession. Sometimes, when we are depressed either we will try and use our obsession to get away from reality, or we will lose interest in it because it no longer gives us pleasure. A change in obsession could also be an indicator. For example, a new interest in a dark or morbid subject, such as types of execution, could be a sign.

Bullying

According to the NAS (2010) publication *B is for Bullied*, over 40 per cent of children on the spectrum have been bullied. If your child is being bullied, it is quite possible that he or she will become depressed. It's important to remember that sometimes children may not tell you that they are being bullied or may not tell you just how bad the bullying is. This may be because they are worried that any intervention might make things worse, or because they don't believe you can do anything to help.

Being uncooperative

When I was depressed, I would sometimes become very uncooperative. I would see no point in doing what was being asked of me, and I didn't care much about upsetting other people. Often it's the family that bears the brunt of this behaviour. If someone starts behaving unreasonably when previously they have been cooperative, it can be a sign that their mood has changed significantly. However, it should also be noted that this could be caused by typical 'teenager-dom'.

Asperger traits becoming more obvious

Sometimes when a person with AS gets depressed, their 'aspieness' becomes more pronounced. They may become more rigid in sticking to a routine, or insist that things are done the 'right' way and get angry if they are not. They may become even less interested in socialising and lose some social skills. Perhaps we just find it harder to keep up our 'neurotypical disguise', or perhaps we just don't have the motivation to keep it going any longer.

Suicide threats

People with Aspergers often mean what they say and say what they mean, so a suicide threat should always be taken seriously. But it's also possible that the threat is the only way that person has of expressing how low they are feeling. Either way these expressions should never be ignored.

Getting upset for no real reason or for unusual reasons

I remember when I was depressed, the smallest thing could make me cry. I remember one night *Top Gear* was delayed by ten minutes because of the snooker and I was in tears for the next hour. If I hadn't been depressed, I would not have got so upset. There can also be a tendency to get really panicky when something goes wrong, or to get furious over something that would previously have just been annoying.

Increased anxiety

For me, anxiety was a big symptom. A tendency to get anxious is normal for people with Asperger syndrome. For example, when I know I am going to be in a new situation I will usually think through every possible problem that might occur and try to come up with solutions. But when I was depressed, the anxiety was far more intense. I would stay up late worrying about every aspect of the next day, including worrying about the fact the day would be even worse because I would be tired, having spent the previous night worrying. These were not my normal Asperger anxieties.

Problems with studies

Depression can affect concentration, making it harder to study. It also makes it more likely that the person will over-react if they encounter a problem with their work. When I was depressed I would sometimes break down in class if I had difficulty with the work. Another person with AS might react with anger and flare up over something that they would previously have dealt with fairly calmly. On the other hand some people become completely apathetic when they are depressed and no longer care about studies, even though previously they had been quite conscientious.

Everyone gets frustrated with studies occasionally or loses interest in work for a while, but a marked change in attitude could indicate that something is wrong.

As you can see, it can be difficult to diagnose depression. The symptoms could be caused by other problems. While these symptoms are all good indicators that *could* support a diagnosis of depression, the best guide is your gut instinct. If you know the person well and you think they may be becoming depressed, then you should *always* take action.

What causes depression?

There are three main schools of thought on the cause of any psychological abnormality, including depression. These are biological, behavioural and cognitive.

Biological approach

The biological approach says that depression is caused by brain chemistry. In our brains, we have various chemicals sloshing around, which aid our brain functioning. Serotonin, noradrenalin and dopamine are three neurotransmitters and low levels of these together with abnormal amounts of other brain chemicals have been found in people with depression. Research has shown that there is a strong link between low levels of these neurotransmitters and depression. However, there is still debate as to whether abnormal brain chemistry causes depression or whether depression causes abnormal brain chemistry.

Behavioural approach

The behavioural approach says that depression is caused by reinforcement. A good example of this would be when I do my maths. If I have a sheet of problems, and keep getting every wrong, it is going to reinforce the idea that I am no good at maths. Experiments have shown that this effect can produce depression (Seligman 1992). Repeated bad experiences can lead to the expectancy of them continuing and a feeling that there is nothing you can do to prevent them.

Cognitive approach

The cognitive approach is similar but more expansive. For example, psychologist Aaron Beck said that depression was caused by wrongful thoughts about the self, the world and the future (Beck *et al.* 1979). So if I get all of the maths questions wrong I would think 'I am useless at maths' → 'I will be useless at everything' → 'I won't get my degree' → 'I am stupid' → 'the world will pity me' → 'I have no future'. As you can see, this quickly leads to very negative thoughts. It is like a snowball being rolled down a snow-laden hillside – it starts small, but it gets bigger and faster. Or, in this case, more negative and more irrational.

Does Asperger syndrome cause depression?

This is a hard question to answer definitively, and one that psychologists are still looking at. It could be that people with AS have a slightly abnormal brain chemistry or brain structure which might result in depression, or perhaps the way people with AS think might make them depression prone. But personally I believe it is the way the world interacts with us that causes depression. Research that my dissertation is based on has found links between depression and autistic traits, but that this effect is largely due to problems in social problem solving – that is, when you control for social problem-solving ability in people with high and low autistic traits, there is little difference in depression. This implies that AS itself does not cause depression, but the social problem-solving issues do.

Teenagers with Asperger syndrome are usually aware that they are different from most other people, and this can be quite isolating. At this age it is particularly important to fit in with one group or another because teenagers are trying to establish an identity independent from their parents. But it also becomes more difficult to fit in; you have to be interested in the right things and wear the right clothes, even use the right kind of language. Anyone who doesn't get it right, even if they get it just slightly wrong, isn't included. And all the rules have to be inferred; no one is going to explicitly tell you how to fit in.

Dealing with depression

It's important to seek help early. If left untreated, depression may begin to have an impact on more and more areas of a person's life, including studies or work. The first step is usually to visit the GP. It can be difficult for someone with AS to talk about how they are feeling. We are often uncomfortable talking about ourselves on a personal level, particularly if we feel vulnerable. We often prefer talking about facts to discussing our emotions and states of mind. For this reason it can be quite helpful to have someone else come with us to the GP who knows us well and can help explain things. The main treatments for depression are medication and talking therapies. I found both of these helpful. However, it's important that any counselling is done by someone who is familiar with autism and understands the way we think. CBT (cognitive behaviour therapy) can work well with people with AS, as it is very structured; however, it does need to be adapted from the normal CBT approach, and some groundwork on understanding emotions may be needed. It also needs to be delivered by someone expert and experienced in both CBT and AS.

MELTDOWNS

'Meltdown' is a term used to describe the situation when, emotionally, we just blow a fuse. In my experience, meltdowns come in three key varieties, which I call 'lockdown', 'contained meltdown' and 'breakout'. Let me talk you through one of my meltdowns.

I'd had a really bad day at school, exams were coming, my grades were going down and things just kept going downhill. The trouble was I let my brain snowball the problem, and so what was just 'bad' became, in my perception, very bad, then awful, then disastrous. This took a few hours to happen, and for a while, I just seemed very quiet. After a time, I started to have a look of despair about me. What then tipped me over the edge was an attempt to do some homework. I found I just couldn't bring myself to do it. I kept trying and failing to get even the first question done. I don't remember much of the next few hours, but things quickly got a lot worse until I had a complete meltdown. I barricaded myself in my room, forced my body into an impossibly small corner and covered myself completely with my duvet. I wanted to hide away from the frustration, the fear and the despair. I was having a panic attack; crying, hyperventilating and shivering. In my head I was going over and over how I was doomed and nothing could help me. This only ended when my parents managed to talk me down. They found the root cause of the panic and tried to find some solutions.

What starts a meltdown?

Fear, anger and despair are the sort of emotions that cause a meltdown, usually as a result of underlying anxiety. Often individuals have a characteristic way of having a meltdown. For example, my brother Jack tends to get very angry when he has a meltdown. This often happens when he is very anxious. I rarely get angry; instead I tend to respond to an overload of anxiety by becoming panicky and overwhelmed. The triggers for a meltdown will vary from person to person, but if their life happens to be in a particularly stressful phase, the meltdowns will be triggered more easily. For example, if I have exams looming I get quite stressed. For other people it may be adjusting to a new environment, such as a new school or class, that puts them under pressure.

I tend to think of us as having two pressure cookers in our head where we store negative experiences. We have a short-term pressure cooker, in which we store the raw emotion that we feel but cannot express. For example, if you get shouted at by your boss, you can't do what you want to do, which is to hit him. Instead you store up that anger in your short-term pressure cooker. And you will feel it for a while, until you have an opportunity to calmly think through what happened and why it happened. This 'thinking through' process takes it out of the short-term pressure cooker but into the long-term pressure cooker. You can remember the incident but you don't really feel anything from it.

Suppose, a few days later, your boss shouts at you again. You go through the same process, privately getting angry (short-term pressure cooker), thinking it through, then storing it in the long-term pressure cooker. The long-term pressure cooker is getting more and more full, hotter and hotter each time this happens, even though you may not actually be aware of this. If the boss shouts at you once too often, the long-term pressure cooker can just boil over, though preferably not at the office. You feel as if you are having a meltdown.

It is also possible for the short-term pressure cooker to boil over, if lots of things go wrong in a short space of time. You don't have the opportunity to think things through in a calm way. Or perhaps you just keep going over and over what happened, getting more and more stressed. If one more thing goes wrong it can easily result in a meltdown. However, long-term meltdowns tend to be worse, and harder to resolve, because they usually involve deeper issues.

Types

As I mentioned earlier, I think there are three types of meltdown – lockdown, contained meltdown and breakout.

Lockdown

A lockdown is a meltdown that shows very few external signs; everything stays locked down in the mind. When I have had them, the most prominent emotion has been despair. I would be totally unresponsive, sometimes hardly aware that people were talking to me. It seemed to take all my energy to keep my state of mind contained. If I had tried to explain or respond I was afraid the feelings would overwhelm me. If there were any outward signs they were shivering or silent crying. Rather than barricading myself in my room, I barricaded myself inside my head, if that makes sense.

Contained meltdown

The contained is the typical meltdown that I described earlier. The behaviour is that of someone trying desperately to hide away. This is usually the longest type of meltdown.

Breakout

A breakout meltdown happens when the anger is so great it cannot be contained and it is targeted outwards, either at one person, at everyone or at objects (for example, by kicking over tables and breaking things). Obviously the person cannot be allowed to be violent towards other people, but sometimes having some kind of physical expression for the anger, such as punching a cushion, can help.

What can you do?

The ideal is to catch a meltdown before it actually happens. Look out for irritability or distracted behaviour. Ask what's been happening, so you will know if there have been any potential triggers during the day. Sometimes it helps to discuss the problem and possible solutions, but if the person is already quite agitated, this can just make things worse.

You could try distraction. For this I would recommend moving to a place where the person feels more comfortable, and getting them to focus on something like a good book, TV programme or movie. Chocolate or some other form of comfort food is good. I have found mashed potatoes, red meat and other stodgy food useful because they make you feel heavy and less panicky. Any favourite food is a good idea. This gives you some time to work out possible ways of dealing with the issue that is threatening to provoke a meltdown. You will then have some good suggestions to make when the person is ready to talk.

If the meltdown has already got under way, then it is unlikely that you will be able to stop it. In this case, a different strategy is needed and it's best to just simply be there for them. There is not much you can do until the body and mind tire themselves out and some rationality is restored. Once the worst is over, it is worth trying to find solutions, as this will help end the meltdown. Afterwards, a good meal (if they can eat), bed, books or TV are recommended to just let the body and mind recover. After a good night's sleep the person will probably be in a better frame of mind to consider any helpful suggestions.

Are meltdowns good?

I know this may sound silly, but I think that sometimes meltdowns are good. Of course they should be averted if possible. But I have found that there are times when I have just had too much long-term stress, and the only way I can get rid of it is to have a meltdown. It is a bit like feeling sick and knowing you will continue to feel sick until you actually throw up. You get it over and done with and you actually feel better afterwards. So while having a meltdown may be hugely distressing for the person and for you, it might also help, as they are getting it out of their system.

ANXIETY

For people with Asperger syndrome, anxiety is pervasive. It is often the driving force behind our behaviour. For example, the bullying I received at school didn't just make me depressed, it made me anxious. I worried about what was going to happen to me tomorrow, about who I might accidentally meet on the street. It had such a profound effect on me that for a year I wouldn't leave the house more than twice a week, and even then I would only go to places where I knew exactly what was going to happen.

There are various ways we handle anxiety, but for many people with AS, anxiety produces a degree of obsessiveness over order. We like to try and make sure that everything happens in the right way. When we discover that despite our best efforts to control everything, stuff still goes wrong, it can result in frustration leading to meltdowns and depression.

Manifestations of anxiety

Meltdowns are fundamentally anxiety issues, and for people with AS, depression usually involves an increase in anxiety. Anxiety is a problem because when we are anxious, we are distracted and therefore less able to function. The way anxiety shows itself in people with AS is often by an increase in aspie traits. For example, I find that when I'm anxious my ability to communication and interact with other people deteriorates. I just don't have the capacity to deal with the anxiety and make eye contact and monitor my body language and make sure you know what I am talking about. It's too much for me.

Often people with AS will become even more rigid in their routines and find any disruption in them difficult. It can also cause us to keep checking and rechecking details to make sure we have things under as much control as possible. For example, Jack gets anxious about going to a respite facility overnight and will phone beforehand to find out who else will be there and which room he will be sleeping in. But it's not enough for Jack to ask these questions once; he has to ask them several times in order to make sure he understood correctly and the answers don't change.

Often there is an increase in repetitive behaviours. When anyone gets stressed it produces agitation and this can be manifested in floor pacing or finger tapping or fidgeting. For aspies the repetitive behaviours are sometimes more noticeable because they are more idiosyncratic. When I am really anxious, I will often start rubbing the back of my neck. I do this without realising it, and it seems to help me release some of the anxious energy. Sometimes the back of my neck has started to bleed because I have been going through a particularly stressful time and just keep doing it. These repetitive behaviours help us deal with the anxiety. It is like letting a bit of pressure out of the pressure cooker. There is still pressure inside it, but it stops us exploding.

Sensory issues, such as sensitivity to sounds or lights, sometimes increase, probably because an increase in anxiety makes us less able to tolerate things that bug us. Sleep difficulties can also worsen, particularly as a result of long-term anxieties such as coping at school.

It's worth noting that some children with AS go to the opposite extreme when they are anxious. For example, if they are being told off they might actually escalate their behaviour so that they seem to become almost giddy with excitement and might start laughing or running around or shouting things out. This is often misinterpreted as deliberately provocative behaviour and the adult in charge gets even more annoyed. This only adds to the child's anxiety and makes them become even more 'high'. It's as if the anxiety is so intolerable for the child that they have to do something – anything – to distract themselves from it.

What can you do to help with anxiety?

A lot depends on the cause of the anxiety and the degree of anxiety being experienced. If the person is worried but not too anxious, it may be possible to talk it through. It often helps to pin down exactly what the person is anxious about. For example, if the person says, 'I'm worried about school lunch tomorrow,' it's helpful to find out exactly what it is about lunch that is a problem. It could be having to eat a particular food, or feeling awkward if they sit on their own, or the general level of noise. Once you understand the causes it may be possible to work out strategies for dealing with them. For example, if the person feels awkward sitting on their own, they could take something to read, or perhaps having a packed lunch would solve some of the problems. Once a general anxiety about school lunch is broken down into specifics and thought through, it can seem less overwhelming.

With some issues, creating a schedule and organising exactly how you are going to tackle the problem can be of great help. Sometimes we try to ignore a problem and don't deal with it until it has become quite bad. At this point it's really helpful to come up with a set plan of action that breaks the issue down into small steps. That way we can start to believe that it's possible to overcome the problem.

If the person with AS is worried about how to manage a new situation, it helps to think about what to do if something goes wrong. For example, suppose your child is worried about travelling by bus on their own. Make a list of the things they are specifically worried about and work out what they should do in each case. Your child might be worried about getting off at the wrong stop, or not having enough money, or missing the bus. Knowing what they should do in each eventuality can help, because then they always have a 'plan B'.

Sometimes anxiety about a new situation is partly caused by the difficulty we have in imagining what it will be like. Photographs of new places and new people help us to build up a picture in our minds. Information about what will happen, when it will happen, where and why is also important, so we know what to expect. If Jack goes on a visit, even if it's a 'fun' visit to a theme park, he likes to know what time we will get there, when we will have lunch, what we will have for lunch, and what time we will leave. It all helps to create an accurate idea of what to expect.

Some anxieties are not easily solved. For example, suppose your child has lost some homework and they have that subject tomorrow. This scenario would have caused a major panic for me when I was at school. It helps to talk through what might happen and how to deal with it. For example, if your child says they've worried because the teacher will be really angry, it helps to work out what the teacher might say, and how your child could respond. The teacher will probably say, 'Where is your homework?!' and your child could say, 'I'm really sorry, I've looked everywhere but I couldn't find it.' It won't stop the teacher being angry (if he or she is angry) but at least your child won't just freeze when it happens and be stuck in a horrible moment. Your child might be worried about getting a detention; it helps to talk through the practical details of what happens in a detention, as sometimes this makes the whole thing a bit less daunting. If your child is still extremely anxious after all this, it might be better to intervene and phone the school to explain the situation.

There is always a balance between how much the person with AS has to live with the environment as it is and tolerate the anxiety, and how much the environment should be altered to alleviate some of the anxiety. I tend to think many people with AS already have high levels of stress from trying to fit in, and if something can be done to reduce it, it's worth doing, especially if the person is getting quite panicky over a particular issue. Think of it as pulling the plug on an electric fan. If you try and stop it working by just holding the blades of the fan, you will probably get some bashed up fingers. If you do manage to hold the blades still, the motor will overheat, causing you more problems. However, if you cut the power, then the blades may keep spinning for a bit, but they will soon stop. It is the same with us.

I mentioned earlier that when I was anxious I would rub the back of my neck. On one occasion I was in a Physics lesson and for some reason I was becoming very anxious. After about 10 minutes I started rubbing the back of my neck. After another 15 minutes, I was aware that my neck was getting painful, but I compulsively kept rubbing it. My support worker, Lea-ann, could see I was getting into a panicky state. She had to decide what to do. She could let things continue as they were, with me getting progressively more anxious and rubbing away the skin on my neck. She could try to stop me from rubbing my neck (which would have been very difficult as it was the only way I could manage the anxiety). Or she could remove me from the situation. She decided (rightly I think) to take me out of the lesson. This was like unplugging the electric fan; the source of anxiety was removed. I was still anxious for a while, but eventually calmed down, though it was hours before I had recovered completely. If she had just made me stop rubbing my neck and stay in the lesson, then my anxiety would have just got worse. I wouldn't have been able to take in what the teacher was saying because I was so stressed.

So how can you 'cut the power' if a person with AS is getting overwhelmed by anxiety? Well, as I just pointed out, removing the person from the situation is one possibility. Going to a known safe area can be very useful. Don't we all have places where we feel safe or associate with being relaxing? For many people it is the bedroom, but unfortunately that is rarely available in day-to-day situations. A small room at school set aside for this purpose is helpful – a comfy chair is really all it needs to be furnished with. Just this simple thing can be really useful.

Another helpful tactic can be telling the person what to do. This may seem odd as you may have found we respond very badly to being told what to do, but this is not always the case. Let me take you back to that Physics lesson I described earlier. I was anxious because I was doing badly and the more anxious I became, the less I was able to follow the lesson. However, I didn't want to leave because if I left, then I would miss more of the teaching and this would make things worse, and it would be my fault. I felt I couldn't stay, but equally I felt I shouldn't go. So I was stuck with a dilemma that I couldn't resolve. However, when my support worker told me to go out (*nicely*) she then took responsibility for any learning I lost. So it wasn't my fault any more, and this meant

I could leave. Sometimes, if you are no longer able to think clearly, it's a relief to have another person take charge.

General destressing tactics that work for the individual are always helpful. Personally, I find that when I need to relax, reading a good book, watching a DVD, or even sometimes doing some maths can be very useful. Why maths? Well, it engages the logical bit of your brain more, and that side is less emotional, and so it can be a good distraction. Also if I'm able to work out the right answers, that gives me a buzz. Other people find Sudoku or crosswords or computer games have the same effect. However, with all of these you need to be careful to make sure that they don't start causing anxiety! It's really useful if the person with AS has an absorbing hobby or, of course, a special interest that gives them a break from everyday pressures. Planning outings or shopping trips related to our interest can help us get through difficult times. Sometimes a physical activity like rowing can help burn off some of the stress.

FINAL THOUGHTS

Among the general population, people who normally manage well can have times when they become quite depressed or anxious or compulsive. In stressful circumstances no one is invulnerable. People with Asperger syndrome are no different, except, perhaps, in the amount of stress they may encounter in their daily lives. Adapting to environments designed by neurotypicals for neurotypicals can be an ongoing challenge. There is no clear dividing line between mental health and mental illness, but a gradation. Most of us have had times when we have felt a bit out of control, or overwhelmed or desperate, and other times when we've felt we're the only sane person around. People who go through these difficult times can recover and in fact deal amazingly well with circumstances others might find very difficult. Often people who have been through a bout of mental illness emerge as more self-aware, compassionate people.

3

THE FIVE SENSES (PLUS TWO)

Here's a simple question for you: how many senses are there? I expect most of you would say that there are five: touch, hearing, vision, taste and smell. But there are actually (technically speaking) a multitude of senses. In addition to the five already mentioned, we are going to look at two other important senses – the proprioceptive sense, which is about awareness of the positioning of your body, and the vestibular sense, which involves balance. These sensory abnormalities are not often discussed, and are not in the current DSM and ICD criteria for autism or Asperger syndrome; however, they have been noted by parents and professionals alike for many years. Indeed, they were even noted by Kanner and Asperger in their original papers.

PROPRIOCEPTIVE SENSE

Proprioception enables your brain to know where the parts of your body are in relation to other parts as you move around. There are sensors on muscles that tell the brain when they are contracting or relaxing. In addition your brain knows from experience how long your legs and arms are. From this, the brain can automatically judge where your body is in relation to itself. It can also judge how much effort to put in to whatever movement you are performing. Try standing with your arms by your sides and eyes shut, then touch the tip of your nose with your finger. The proprioceptive sense enables you to do this and not end up poking yourself in the eye.

VESTIBULAR SENSE

In the inner part of the ear there are three semicircular canals. These are used by the brain to manage balance, which is a central part of the vestibular system. However, this system doesn't work perfectly. For example, if you stand on one leg, you will probably be able to balance without much difficulty. However, if you try to stand on one leg with your eyes closed, you will find it much harder to keep your balance. This is because the vestibular system is aided by vision. That is why, if you are up a ladder and afraid of heights, it is still a good idea to keep your eyes open.

So we have established seven senses. So what? Why should these senses be particularly important for people with Asperger syndrome? Well, people on the autistic spectrum are often subject to hypersensitivity, hyposensitivity or other sensory problems.

HYPERSENSITIVITY

With hypersensitivity, one or more of the senses is much more acute than normal. For example, I know someone who can hear very minor microphone feedback. It is so minor that most people don't hear it. But he does hear it and it can prove intensely annoying, especially as he goes to a lot of conferences. Another example would be hypersensitivity to light. I often find myself looking down when I walk outside simply because of the brightness. If I look straight ahead when the sun is shining, then this is usually too bright for me. I find that very uncomfortable. Lying back on the grass on a sunny day and looking up at the clouds would be impossible for me to do because of the glare of the sun.

HYPOSENSITIVITY

Hyposensitivity means that a person does not get much sensory impact from one or more of their senses. This makes them crave bright lights or loud sounds or strong flavours. Sometimes these children love extreme theme park rides. They need the buzz and excitement in order to feel really alive. A classic example would be a small boy who is hyposensitive to sound setting off the school fire alarm just to get the sensory input he desires. It's a bit like having really bunged up ears – everything seems quieter and you experience a kind of auditory numbness. It's really annoying when that happens, isn't it? You really want to hear loud and clear, to have some vivid auditory sensations. This is just what this boy is doing – getting that extra input he desires.

CAUSES OF HYPERSENSITIVITY AND HYPOSENSITIVITY

What causes hyper- and hyposensitivities? Well, let's think a bit about how we perceive things. Right now, are you aware of the sensations in your feet, the feel of the socks and shoes you are wearing? You will probably say yes (and realise how hot and sticky they are!). But you probably only became aware of the sensation when you focused your attention on your feet. Prior to that your brain filtered out that information because it wasn't important. But what if your brain didn't have this filtering system? The thought, 'My feet are hot and sticky!' would keep popping into your head. This would get quite irritating and distracting so that after a while you would really want to take your shoes off. With hypersensitivity, the brain lets in too much sensory input, and doesn't disregard enough of it.

Hyposensitivity is the exact opposite, and the brain's filtering system is blocking out too much. Have you ever been at the beach and had to walk over some really jagged stones in bare feet in order to get to the water? It can be quite painful. But as you gingerly make your way to the water, there is usually a little boy who will run full pelt over the same stones, intent on getting in the water as quickly as possible, and quite oblivious to any pain messages from his feet. He is showing hyposensitivity.

CHANGEABILITY

An individual may be prone to hypersensitivity but it can vary, depending on circumstances and their mood. If I'm having a bad day, I have noticed that I tend to look down more and I tend to find loud noises even louder. This is not coincidence, it is due to how I am feeling. All my energy and concentration is taken up with day-to-day stresses, so sudden loud noises startle me more and make me feel overloaded. Do the kids seem too noisy when you come home after a bad day at work? It is the same thing. This may also be true of hyposensitivity. If a person is stressed out, they may want the distraction of a really loud, exciting environment. Or alternatively, if the hyposensitive person has been in a very boring, bland environment for too long, they may be desperate for some excitement. They may find it very hard to tolerate dullness.

A BIT OF PSYCHOLOGY

There are two theories in psychology that are particularly relevant to hyper- and hyposensitivities. First the Yerkes-Dodson Law, which relates physiological arousal to information processing. In short, it says that with low arousal, there will be low information processing (i.e. not really paying attention, not noticing the stimuli), at medium arousal, there will be optimum information processing, and at high arousal, there will be low information processing (i.e. too much going on, cannot focus). It is quite easy to see how sensory input relates to this law – too much or too little sensory input, and it can disrupt processing – whether this be work or social situations.

The second psychological concept I want to introduce you to is habituation. Let's say your neighbours suddenly decide to put a shooting range in their back garden. The first time you hear a gunshot, you are likely to jump out of your skin. However, over time, you get used to it, you start to expect it. You have become habituated to it. Most animals show this same process. Sometimes people on the spectrum do not show habituation. We do not get used to something over time. The last time we hear the school bell, we are just as scared or surprised as we were the first time.

HYPERSENSITIVE AND HYPOSENSITIVE BEHAVIOUR
Touch

Suppose a child always seems to kick off the duvet, even on the coldest night. If the child is hypersensitive to touch, then the tiny bobbles that form on a duvet cover when it has been washed lots of times may be intensely irritating. Alternatively the child may have a hyposensitivity to cold and just not be particularly aware of any discomfort when the duvet falls off. Or perhaps you have bought a new duvet cover (because of the bobbling) and it feels different. For us a seemingly minor change can have a really major effect. Have you ever gone to a hotel and found it harder to sleep because it is a different mattress? Or because there are unusual sounds outside? For us, a new duvet cover can seem an equally disconcerting change.

The same logic applies to clothes. Have you ever worn new shoes and noticed that they feel a bit uncomfortable until they have been 'worn in'? After a few wearings they soften up and mould more to the shape of your foot. For us both new shoes and new clothes can feel uncomfortable and strange. This may explain why a lot of people with AS are only at ease if they wear the same clothes every day. Often we have half a dozen T-shirts or jumpers which are identical. This also makes getting dressed in the morning more simple.

A lot of people with AS have an aversion to doing messy things and this tends to be most noticeable with children, because they are expected to enjoy things like finger painting, using clay and getting muddy on the football field. My youngest brother Jordan likes doing crafts but hates getting glue on his fingers. He likes cooking but not mixing things with his hands. Being messy results in feeling very odd sensations and these are sensations you cannot easily get rid of because there is stuff actually on your hands. The only way to remove it is to wash it off. Other children seem able to ignore the 'ick' factor of messy tasks, or even relish it. For us it just feels rather disgusting.

Walking on tiptoes is quite common in very young children with autism. One reason might be because they find the arch of their feet very sensitive. Try taking your shoes and socks off and running a feather over your arch, it's very sensitive to touch. Equally, a lot of people on the spectrum do not like being touched because of the sensory component to it, as well as the social component.

What about hyposensitivity? Here we can see the reverse of the 'ick' factor, and loving to touch and play with food, clay, paint, etc., as it is a different sensation. Sometimes there is a lack of awareness of the temperature outside, and so we might run into snow with only a T-shirt on.

Pain

Although pain is technically a slightly different sense, I will mention it here. Some people on the spectrum seem to have an extremely high tolerance for pain, and can break bones or badly cut themselves and not take any notice of it. This is uncommon, but worth mentioning, particularly as it can make it harder to tell if children have seriously hurt themselves.

Hearing

Sound sensitivity is very common in people with AS. I am slightly hypersensitive to sound, which means that sudden loud noises can be really hard for me to deal with. Every time the bell rang at my school, I felt like I was jumping out of my skin. Imagine it happening right next to your ear when you are asleep – it would give you quite a shock, wouldn't it? It was like that for me every time the school bell went off. Having said that, this does not mean we cannot cope with all loud noise. For example, at university, I am part of the Ents Crew, who set up sound and lights for university events such as discos and concerts. During the events I am often in the thick of things with music blaring out at around 85–95 decibels; when I am DJing, I am exposed to 100 decibels. But this is not a problem for me because the music is predictable and constant and I can adjust to it. The music is not a sudden sharp sound. Others who are hypersensitive may not be able to cope with this though. I know someone who will find a slightly loud environment really painful and will have to leave quickly – it is that excruciating.

Sound hypersensitivity may also account for the reluctance of some children with AS to attend events that most children enjoy. Parties where there is a lot of noise can be difficult, and cinemas often have the sound very loud. Fun events where there is a lot of loud music can be a problem as can pantomimes where the children are expected to shout out responses. Sudden loud noises can be quite frightening for younger children with AS. Often they are less good at anticipating when a loud noise will happen, and when it does it can give them quite a shock. However, as they mature they become better at coping with it. Jordan used to have a real problem with any kind of group shouting, but now he just sticks his fingers in his ears and shouts with the rest of them. Sometimes earplugs can be very useful, particularly if your child wants to do something but is worried about the noise. Jack uses them in the cinema, and at a firework display no one is going to notice if you have earplugs in. I particularly recommend professional sound engineer earplugs, as they give a good seal, and dampen sound frequencies equally, so things generally sound the same.

People with sound hypersensitivity can find it hard to disguise their strong reactions. Jack immediately reacts angrily if he is startled by a sudden loud noise, which can be a problem in public. This kind of reaction can get the person with AS into trouble (for example, in a classroom setting) or leave them vulnerable to teasing if other people deliberately try to cause a big reaction by making sudden loud noises.

Vision

Quite a few people with Asperger syndrome and autism seem to have a sensitivity to bright contrasts and flashing lights. For example, I sometimes see fluorescent lights as lights that flash very quickly, which gives me a headache. Other people find that some flashing lights make them feel nauseous. This seems to be particularly caused by lights that flash quickly in the dark, strobe lighting being a classic example. When visual hypersensitivity particularly affects reading, it is sometimes described as 'scotopic sensitivity syndrome'. Words appear to be shimmering, moving, double printed or blurred. This can be worse when the page is brightly lit (for example, strong sunlight) particularly if the print is very dark and the paper very white. Fortunately I am not affected by this, but I know several people who find it quite difficult to deal with. Imagine having to read this book, when every word seems to be jiggling and moving about. It would be difficult to keep reading, and would probably give you a headache. Children with this sensitivity often find learning to read more difficult, and may not think to comment on the way the words seem to shimmer because they think that's the way everyone sees the words.

Some people have found that the use of tinted plastic overlaid on the text being read can be beneficial. I remember I was tested and given one of these filters. While it didn't often do much good, it was sometimes useful when I was having difficulty concentrating. Some people go further and have tinted glasses so they see the whole world through that specific tint. These glasses are known as Irlen lenses. They are usually only used in cases when the scotopic sensitivity is not limited to reading and writing, but affects their sight generally. I haven't found the use of tinted materials particularly effective, but I know several people who have.

Taste and smell

Many children with AS are fussy eaters and this may be due to taste and smell sensitivities. A lot of how we taste actually comes from our sense of smell, meaning hypersensitivity or hyposensitivity in either of these areas could produce problems with eating. Sometimes foods with a strong taste or smells that linger, such as garlic, onions or pepperoni, are a particular problem. Alternatively, if the child is hyposensitive, they may really enjoy hot spicy foods, and strong flavours. The texture of food can also be significant. Jack will eat spaghetti but not other types of pasta. Lots of children and adults with AS would happily eat the same meal every day, as it means there is a smaller set of tastes to get used to; however, it can also result in a rather restricted diet. It should be noted that this behaviour could also be due to having a food routine which they do not want broken, rather than disliking other foods. Often for hypersensitive tasters, food that is disliked will cause a very strong response (as in 'Yuck! That's disgusting!'), and this can be a bit tricky in social situations.

Proprioception

A minority of people with autism have an amazing ability to climb and balance, and this may be due to hypersensitive proprioception. Many people with AS are more awkward physically and movements lack ease and fluidity. For example, they may have a stiff, almost robotic walk or a tendency to turn the whole body to look at something, rather than just moving the head and eyes. This may be due to hyposensitive proprioception, which makes it hard to know where your body is, and can lead to some rather embarrassing and painful accidents. Something as simple as walking on a flat carpet could result in tripping up. Other small things like doing up the zip on a coat or catching a ball can be tricky because of the coordination needed. If movement problems are causing significant difficulties, the person could be dyspraxic (see Chapter 7). People with hyposensitivity may actually enjoy the stimulation of jumping on a trampoline or swinging because of the strong forces being exerted on the body.

EFFECTS

A change in how we perceive the world is clearly going to have an important impact on how we behave. If our world is brighter, or quieter, or smellier than yours, we are going to respond differently to things – our behaviour will be affected. This is important to remember when trying to work out why someone on the spectrum did something. A common example is lashing out at someone at school for no apparent reason. It could be that the school bell has just gone off, which, for someone with a hypersensitivity to noise, can be utterly terrifying, and trigger a 'fight or flight' response. It is not an excuse for hitting someone, but it is an explanation as to why the behaviour might have occurred. Alternatively, the person might have a hypersensitivity to touch, and so someone bumping into them could feel more aggressive than it actually is.

4

STIMMING, OBSESSIONS AND RITUALS

Some of Our More Noticeable Behaviour Explained

One of the most commonly noticed behaviours of someone with Asperger syndrome is the presence of an obsession, or – as I often call them – a specialist subject. Others might notice odd habits, such as always wearing the same old jumper indoors, even when it is hot. Someone with AS may have certain rituals, like making a cup of tea while reciting the instructions their mum gave them when they first learned to make one. It's also possible that a person with AS might also have an odd habit, such as humming or hand flapping, otherwise known as a 'stim'. This chapter is going to take a look at all three types of behaviour and explore the reasons why we do them. We'll also look at whether they need to be controlled, and how to do that.

STIMMING

The word 'stim' is short for stimming or sensory self-stimulation, and refers to short, repetitive movements or vocalisations. Originally the term tended to be used to describe the movements severely autistic people sometimes make, such as rocking or twirling. It was thought that these movements were made because the person enjoyed the sensory stimulation. Since then the term has come to refer to any repetitive movement which serves no functional purpose. For most people with AS it is actually something that helps them calm down and/or concentrate rather than something that stimulates them. Asperger-type examples are hand flapping, leg jiggling, bum clenching, humming a particular note, or making fish-like mouth movements. However, stimming is by no means limited to this. Different children will stim in very different ways, and it is important to keep an open mind as to what could be a stim. My own stim is to rub the back of my neck. If you see me doing it you know I'm getting somewhat stressed. There are some good examples of stimming behaviour (along with other sensory behaviours) in Amanda Baggs' YouTube video called *In My Language*.

The tendency to stim can be almost automatic. Often we don't even realise we are doing it. For example, I have a friend studying at Cambridge whose leg jiggles when she is concentrating hard. This is fine when she is working at home or revising for an exam – but in an exam hall it can be very distracting for others. If she is asked to stop, all she can think about is that she mustn't jiggle her leg. And as soon as she starts concentrating on her work again her leg starts jiggling. It's something she does without being aware of it.

Why do we stim?

There can be many reasons for this – it will vary from person to person. However, I know for me it helps me calm down just a little bit when I'm getting stressed. It takes the edge off some of the anxious energy. Like a safety pressure valve, when I get too stressed, stimming lets out some of the pressure. I often use the analogy of a bottle of fizzy drink. Throughout the day there may be lots of small problems, each of which makes me slightly more anxious, or shakes the bottle a bit more. By the end of the day there is a lot of pressure that has accumulated inside the bottle. If you unscrew the cap just a little, so you get a small release of pressure – this helps to make sure the bottle doesn't explode! In the same way if I'm feeling quite pressured because the stress is building up, rubbing the back of my neck seems to ease things a bit. It's as if the anxious part of my brain can express the tension by stimming, which allows the rest of my brain to focus and concentrate on the task in hand.

Sometimes a stim starts as a response to stress, but over time it becomes a habit. For example, students may start drinking coffee to keep themselves awake late into the night in order to revise for exams. They may keep drinking coffee when they are working after the exams have finished, because it has become a habit. It is the same thing for us. We may start stimming because we are stressed, but over time we may just stim when we are working or in a potentially stressful situation. It simply becomes a habit.

There are times when people with AS do want the sensory stimulation they get from stimming. Try flapping your hands for 60 seconds. You'll get a funny feeling when you are doing it, and another strange feeling when you have stopped. Sometimes we do it to get that sensory feedback from the rush of blood and from the nerves associated with touch. The same could be said of spinning around. Getting dizzy is an interesting sensation, especially when you stop suddenly and your surroundings seem to keep spinning. I went through a phase where I would pinch my nose, keep my mouth shut, and try to blow out. This caused my ears to do something funny, so that when I hummed it would sound really loud, which I found kind of soothing.

At other times stimming can result from excitement, particularly for children. When something really good happens, it's a fairly normal reaction to want to jump up and punch the air (watch a football crowd when a goal is scored) or perhaps to clap (at a cricket match). Some children with Aspergers will express their delight or excitement by jumping up and down a lot, and/or clapping and hand flapping.

Stimming can also be a coping mechanism. As I mentioned earlier, I sometimes rub the back of my neck to relieve stress. When I was going through a particularly stressful time, I would sometimes start to rub harder and faster even to the point when it got a bit painful. It was a way of removing my mental focus from the stressor for a few moments. For a person with AS, the strain of having to act 'normal' can be enormous. Sometimes under pressure we temporarily forget our acting skills and that's when some of these aspie mannerisms start to show through.

So is stimming a good thing?

Stimming does help some people with AS to concentrate, just as anyone in the general population might doodle or fiddle with a pen when they are thinking hard. It's almost like a distraction for the distractible part of the brain, enabling the rest of the brain to stay focused. The stims that people with AS have are sometimes just a bit more idiosyncratic. For many of us, if we can't stim then we will be unable to concentrate.

On the down side, our stimming may affect the concentration of other people, if it's distracting for them. This can be a problem in exam situations. If I keep rubbing the back of my neck in an exam, no one is going to notice, but sometimes I hum on one note in order to concentrate. Fortunately I am allowed to take my exams away from other students, so I don't need to worry about this. Stimming can annoy other people in a class situation and may also result in teasing or bullying.

There is also the possibility that too much stimming could prove harmful. Too much hand flapping could damage the wrist joint, and teeth grinding can do damage to the surface of teeth. Also, if the stimming habit takes over too much, it can become a way of just tuning out and dissociating. If the stimming is beginning to interfere with normal life it's usually an indication that the person is becoming very stressed.

In fact an increase in stimming can be a useful indication of the amount of anxiety a person is experiencing. For example, my key worker at college knew that if she saw me frantically rubbing the back of my neck, then she needed to take me out of class and calm me down. However, it is important to remember that not all stims are a response to stress. Sometimes they just show that the person is concentrating and sometimes they are simply for pleasure. In this case they may just indicate that your child is in a good mood or is really enjoying a particular activity. The important thing is to learn to differentiate between stims that are positive, stims that are negative and those that are neutral. This will become more apparent once you begin to notice where and when the person stims.

But suppose the stimming is causing problems. Perhaps it looks a bit weird and is making other people uncomfortable. Or maybe classmates have begun to notice and are teasing or getting irritated. Should the stimming then be stopped? My answer to this is a resounding *No!* Why? Remember the fizzy drink analogy. Imagine your child is a bottle of fizzy drink, coping with the daily stresses of living in a world that can be confusing and difficult to predict. Throughout the day your child will getting stressed. Perhaps they were late for a class, then had trouble trying to understand what was required for homework, then had problems with the other kids at break time. Each of these will shake up the metaphorical bottle. If you don't let your child stim and let out a bit of pressure from the bottle, then that bottle will explode and they will have a meltdown. Not only that, but if you try to forbid stimming, you will be adding stress while taking away the means of coping with it. You will also be limiting your ability to gauge their mood. So what can you do? The answer is not to stop stimming, but to change it.

Changing stimming

Let me give you an example of how we can change stimming. Tapping the table with my fingers can be very annoying and distracting for others. What if instead I tapped my leg? Suddenly the sound changes and the noise is reduced. I still have the same movement but it is much quieter. Another alternative would be to get a small sponge on which to tap. This virtually eliminates the noise.

What about hand flapping? Well, you could try getting the child to slow the movement down and to restrict it to their fingers. This makes the movement less conspicuous and probably less distracting for others. But if it is the sensory buzz the child misses, then they may not get the same pleasure or stress relief from this modified version. What then? If the child just needs the release of stimming, perhaps instead of stimming during lessons they could be let out of lessons at regular intervals in order to have a short burst of stimming. However, as I mentioned earlier, a stim is something that we often do without realising it, so at first the child may unintentionally slip back into stimming in class. In this case, gentle kind reminders may help. Some children respond well to reward charts, collecting a star for, say, each half hour during which they manage to avoid stimming. If they collect enough stars they get a small reward. However, this can cause frustration if the child tends to stim accidentally.

It's important not to punish stimming. This just creates more pressure for the individual, and increases the need to stim. Flexibility and sensitivity are also important. Take the example of trying to train someone to tap on their leg instead of tapping on the table. On a good day, if they start inadvertently tapping on the table, kind reminders and praise may work. But if they are having a bad day, it's probably best to not to persist. The aim is to change the stim gradually without creating additional pressure. Change should be done through rewarding when they do keep it to set times or do it in a different way, not by punishing when they don't.

OBSESSIONS

One of the well-known characteristics of autistic spectrum disorders is a tendency to have obsessions. An obsession is a topic that fascinates you, that you think about all the time. You want to know every detail, every fact, every line in every episode, every statistic – you want to know everything about it. I prefer to call obsessions 'specialist subjects' as this seems a more positive description. It's actually no bad thing to have an overriding interest in something. Most people have hobbies and projects. These specialist subjects have a wide range of manifestations, and change over time. For example, Jack is 18 and has so far had these specialist subjects: Thomas the Tank Engine, *The Simpsons*, Pokémon characters, heights of celebrities, days and dates, dinosaurs, countries, flags and Sonic the Hedgehog. There are probably more, I just can't remember them all! I have noticed that as he gets older his interest in a topic lasts even longer. At the moment my obsession seems to be psychology, autism, Asperger syndrome and DVDs – and I hope the interest in psychology lasts for at least another year as I'm studying it for my degree!

So why do we have obsessions? In my opinion we have them because we have a desire for control. For us the world around us is quite a scary place. We don't understand how you can seem to communicate without words, we cannot understand your social rules and body language. To you the world is safe, and generally predictable. We are always at a disadvantage. For us everything is more unexpected and random. But in our specialist subjects we are the experts. We can gradually build our knowledge, finding out each detail, and working out how it all fits together. We can draw up lists, compare and classify, uncover the rules and the exceptions to the rules. It's satisfying to feel that there is one area of life we have completely mastered.

Childhood obsessions often have a strong visual element and involve collections of things. TV series such as *Thomas the Tank Engine, Pokémon* and *Yu-Gi-Oh!* are common examples. You can watch the programmes and collect the model engines or the cards or the plastic figures. Cards often contain lots of data so they can be classified and ordered in various ways, and children can learn all the details. Figures and models can be lined up and put in order. Other obsessions often involve powerful machines; cars, tractors and aeroplanes are popular. Sometimes children have more unusual specialisms such as petrol stations, vacuum cleaners or types of phone mast. Teenagers with AS often become interested in table-top war games such as Warhammer 40,000. They often meet up at games workshops where they can often paint the miniature figures they buy, and meet with fellow enthusiasts. Science fiction is another popular obsession in this age group.

Some of the obsessions with particular TV series may also stem from an urge to try to understand people in an easy, non-threatening way. For us the social world seems quite unpredictable. For many people, arachnophobia is due to the sudden, fast and unpredictable movement of spiders. For us, you are equally unpredictable in what you are going to do, and what you do happens equally quickly and suddenly. Watching certain TV series gives us a basic insight into emotions and interactions, and a better chance at predicting your behaviour. However, more importantly, a video or DVD never changes – it is completely predictable. For example, in *Thomas the*

Tank Engine the faces of the engines show emotions very clearly, and the reasons for them feeling the emotions are obvious (the learning component). Thomas wins a race so he is happy, Henry loses a race so he is cross. Children with an ASD will often watch the same episode, and even the same section of an episode, over and over again, so they know exactly what will happen and why (the predictability component). The cartoon series enjoyed by older children (*Pokémon, Sonic the Hedgehog, Yu-Gi-Oh!*) have simple social situations, such as a group of friends on a quest. The faces are drawn with big eyes which exaggerate the emotional expression, making them easy to understand. I watch the same episodes of *The West Wing, Star Trek* and *Friends* (to name a few) over and over again. It helps me understand all the motivations, and all the reasoning behind the characters' emotions. I'm then better at working out people's motivations in real life, and I can make more sense of their emotions. I can play back a bit of an episode until I really understand it, so I can then apply it to similar real life situations.

Obsessions also can provide a form of escapism. You can escape to a world where you can use your imagination and have total control. The more facts you know about your specialist subject, the more detailed the created world becomes. If you have ever read a good novel, you will probably agree it is the little details which really bring it to life. Most people can become absorbed in the imaginative world of a good book but people with AS often find this difficult. It involves understanding the feelings of the characters, and their motivations. But specialist subjects enable us to escape from a reality that is sometimes confusing and difficult. It's interesting that we will often take refuge in this when under stress. Children with AS will sometimes start reciting information about their specialist subject when they are a bit stressed. It's as if it provides a safe haven and a welcome distraction.

There can also be some element of pure curiosity. We are by nature curious creatures, and channelling that curiosity is natural. You may channel it by reading this book and learning a bit about Asperger syndrome, someone else may watch documentaries. Most people will have several outlets for their curiosity, but with

Aspergers or autism, there is often just one overriding outlet – the specialist subject.

So are obsessions good?

Yes, they can be. A specialist subject can be used as a motivator for children with AS. For example, time spent on a specialist subject can be used as a reward, as can new plastic figures or collector cards, or a visit to a favourite place relevant to the specialist subject. Learning can sometimes be constructed to involve the specialist subject. If a child is obsessed with Thomas the Tank Engine, a maths problem, such as 5−2+4, can become:

> 'Thomas was given a special job. He had to deliver logs to the other side of the island. He started out with five logs, but on the way two fell off. At the next station he collected four more logs. How many logs will he deliver to the other side of the island?'

If as parents and teachers you can be creative with our specialist subjects, you may find you can tap into that curiosity and enthusiasm. Admittedly not every specialist subject can be used in this way, and not every area of the curriculum lends itself to this kind of adaptation. But it's an idea that sometimes works really well. We all learn more when we are interested. How much do you know about your favourite TV show? It's much easier to engage with something when it's related to our particular interests.

Sometimes the kind of thinking involved in learning about a specialist subject comes into its own in secondary school. In some subjects, such as the various branches of science, there is an awful lot of fact-learning and ordering according to various principles. This is just the kind of thing that an aspie is good at. Information technology involves remembering lots of details and figuring out how things work. Again, this is often something in which a person with AS excels.

As people progress through secondary school they are required to specialise more, and this works to the advantage of someone with Asperger syndrome. We can drop the subjects that we find more difficult, such as PE and English Literature, and focus in on the things we are good at. I didn't do particularly well at GCSEs but I did much better at A levels when I was only studying subjects I liked, including my specialism, Psychology. Even if a specialist subject is not academic, it may provide a career opportunity.

Professor Tony Attwood once told a story of a young boy with Asperger syndrome whose school insisted he do work experience like everyone else. So they called in Tony Attwood, who talked to the boy and asked what he enjoyed, and he answered fishing. He loved fishing, he knew where each type of fish could be caught, what type of bait to use, what rod, what line, everything. Tony suggested he do work experience at a fishing tackle shop. And so it was arranged and the week he spent there passed, and then Tony got a call from the school, and the school said that work experience went well, in fact it went so well he hadn't left. The shop loved him as he knew so much and could really help customers, the customers loved him for the same reason, and he liked working there because he could get little bits of knowledge from others, but best of all, he was surrounded by people who found him and his skill useful. He went on to get a full-time job there. So clearly specialist subjects can be useful (Attwood 2001).

Another positive aspect of having an obsession is that it can promote friendships with like-minded individuals. Lots of aspies hate making small talk and don't particularly enjoy socialising for its own sake. But if they find other people who share their enthusiasm for a particular interest, socialising suddenly becomes easy. It's probably worth looking out for relevant clubs and interest groups as these will probably work better than broader-based groups such as cubs, scouts or youth groups.

On the other hand, obsessions aren't always good. The two main problems are inappropriate obsessions and obsessions which become too important. Inappropriate obsessions might include obsessions with morbid subjects, such as methods of execution or weapons, and obsessions which other people may find offensive, such as pornography. A lot depends on the age of the individual. There is a fair argument that when someone is approaching adulthood, they have a right to choose their own interests, as long as they don't inflict them on other people. However, sometimes a new preoccupation with a morbid subject can indicate an unhappy state of mind. It seems that if a person starts to get worried about, for example, death and dying, they want to find out all about it, perhaps in the hope of somehow reducing their own anxiety. But instead, the more they find out, the more the topic dominates their thinking.

An interest in combat and weaponry could be fairly innocent, but if the person starts collecting weapons this could invite suspicion. Similarly it's fine to have an interest in the SAS but if you roam the streets at night wearing a black balaclava, this may be misinterpreted. At a certain age it's natural to have an interest in sexual development and reproduction, but it causes problems if your child inflicts their special interest on other people by asking them personal questions. A special interest may cause the person to behave inappropriately towards strangers. It's fine to be interested in, say, mobile phones, but it isn't fine to approach a stranger who is using a mobile phone and ask to look at it.

How do you judge if an obsession is becoming too important? If it's beginning to control family life it's clearly a problem. If your child has a major tantrum when you don't visit the shop every Saturday to buy another item for their collection, sooner or later it's going to be an issue. Similarly, if their obsession is causing them to act inappropriately with other people, for example by approaching strangers, it may make them vulnerable. Or, with a teenager, if their specialist interest is controlling their own life to the extent that they are neglecting schoolwork and spending hours on end alone in their room, they may need some controls put in place. Having said that, it's not unusual for any teenagers to spend hours in their room neglecting their schoolwork, so in the end it's a matter of personal judgement!

One special interest which may pose particular problems is a fascination with violent computer games or violent TV programmes and films. Most teenagers who play these or watch these tend to become a bit desensitised to the way real people feel when subjected to real acts of violence. Their empathy becomes blunted. Violence may have even more effect on people with AS, as they have pre-existing difficulties in understanding how other people feel. Some people with AS also have more difficulty distinguishing between reality and the version of reality seen in these games and films. Most people who watch them or play them are aware that people don't behave like that in real life, but this distinction may be less obvious to some people with an ASD. For example, Jack would probably laugh if he saw someone trip over in the street, because he isn't aware of the distinction between slapstick comedy (he loves Mr Bean) and real life. Others with an ASD may have no difficulties in this area, and many are very caring, but it can be an issue.

How do we control obsessions that have become problematic?

This can be quite difficult as the obsessions are usually very strong. However, there are a few strategies which you can try.

The first is to assign times for it when your child can pursue their obsession. This uses the AS love of having a schedule. You do need to be sensitive to the individual's current routine and the purpose the special interest serves within that. For example, it may seem like a really good idea to stipulate 'Homework first, then you can do your special interest.' But it may be that the reason the person wants to indulge in their obsession as soon as they get home from school is that they need to unwind before they can attempt to focus on homework. It's a bit like you coming in from a hard days' work. Perhaps all you want to do at that point is to sit down with a cup of tea and do the Sudoku. Or after dinner, maybe all you want to do is to put your feet up and watch *EastEnders* before getting the kids ready for bed. You do it to treat yourself or give yourself a break. If you had to get everything done before you had a chance to relax, you would just get very irritable. Maybe the best compromise is to allow a specific amount of time for the special interest straight after school – for example, 45 minutes every day – and then expect the homework to be tackled after that. We aspies don't like change or feeling we are losing control so before instigating any change, it's important to talk it through with your child and take their views into account. Then allow some time for them to adjust their expectations before beginning the new regime. On a practical level, if you are dealing with a child it may help to use a timer for the 45 minutes. That way they can see how many minutes they have left, rather than being surprised when told that time's up.

If an obsession is inappropriate, you could try broadening it out to include more acceptable areas. For example, you could try broadening an interest in sexual development to include more general human biology or reproduction in different species of animals. Or you could encourage a person who is fascinated by weapons to become interested in the history of weaponry. The aim is to subtly change the focus of the special interest so there is less concentration on dubious material. However, it may be that part of the attraction of an obsession is the excitement of it being a slightly forbidden, 'grown-up' subject, in which case trying to make it more acceptable may not work.

One alternative is to try to replace an obsession with something completely different. For children it's good to choose something that has some credibility in the playground. For example, knowledge of football teams and players works well, particularly if there are football cards to collect. Often there is a current craze, perhaps linked to a TV series, and if your child can be interested in that it helps them socially. Teenagers are not easily influenced, but if your child has an obsession that you feel uncomfortable about, it's a good idea to watch for any interest in other areas and try to encourage that. For example, if they begin to show an interest in a particular TV programme, you could get the series on DVD. It's sometimes easier to change an obsession before it begins to take hold, or when it's beginning to lose its appeal.

You could always try just explaining that the obsession is inappropriate and insist that they abandon it, but this is unlikely to work well. Imagine you were told you couldn't watch a favourite TV programme any more. You would probably feel quite angry and resentful, particularly if you didn't agree with the reasons for the ban. Or you would submit and then get quite stressed, having been deprived of the enjoyment and relaxation you gained from watching it. You might even secretly continue watching and just get used to deceiving other people. Whichever course you took, life would probably seem that bit harder as a result. A fairer approach might be to just tell your child that other people feel uncomfortable about their obsession so it needs to be kept private. Or explain that other people are now completely bored by the obsession so it's best if they don't keep talking about it *all* the time.

RITUALS AND RIGIDITY

Many people with AS can be a bit rigid in their behaviour. We often have a certain way of doing a particular thing, which we like to stick with at all costs. For example, I had to keep home and school separate when I was at secondary school. So I would always try and do all my homework while I was actually in school, working in the library during break times and the lunch hour. This meant that I didn't get the chance to eat during the school day; it was just more important to me to get the work finished. Sometimes there was too much homework and I had to take it home with me. If this happened, I wouldn't change out of my uniform, or eat or drink, or even use the bathroom until it was all done. I had to complete the homework on the day it was set. I couldn't leave some of it until the next day, even if I knew I would have time to do it then. It was only when all the work was done that I could relax, get changed and have something to eat. My rigid thinking ('I *must* get the work finished before I can take a break') resulted in the ritual of doing things in this particular way. It was my way of managing the stresses of school life, and I didn't want to risk changing it.

When I was at primary school, I didn't get on well with the other kids. Break times were awkward because I wasn't asked to join in games, and even if I had been I wouldn't have enjoyed it. However, I hated just standing there, not knowing what to do. I noticed there were coloured lines painted on the asphalt showing the different pitches for football and netball, and I started to walk along them. It gave me something to do and made me feel less conspicuous. So every break time that is what I would do – just walk along the lines. I also found that if wore my anorak with the hood over my head and the zipper zipped right up (with just my nose poking out) I didn't notice the other children, so this too became part of the ritual. Ironically this ended up making me more conspicuous because I would wear the anorak like that even on hot summer days. It was the way I coped with the playtime difficulties, and even though it had its disadvantages (such as feeling faint in the 30 degree heat!) I preferred to stick with it, rather than risk trying to find different ways of coping.

Sometimes the rigid behaviour isn't the result of needing to find a way of managing with an ongoing difficulty. It's more the result of a habit which has become a ritual that mustn't be changed. Jack likes watching *The Simpsons* and we always have to watch it at 6pm on Channel 4. Jack has seen most episodes several times, and has them on DVD, so he could watch them whenever he wanted. However, he still insists that we have *The Simpsons* on at that time every day, even though he sometimes doesn't actually sit and watch it. In fact the ritual has become more elaborate because Jack has a friend at his school who also likes *The Simpsons*. Jack phones this friend every day after the episode to read to him the synopsis of the plot, which he finds on the internet. I think his friend has probably just watched the episode himself, but for some reason it's really important to both of them that they do this. If we stopped Jack from doing it, he would get very agitated and angry.

Everyone likes to feel they can anticipate roughly what will happen on a day-to-day basis. But most people also enjoy the flexibility or being able to do something different They can think of various possibilities and choose between them. But some people with an ASD find it very difficult to think up possibilities, because of the imaginative impairment. They need to stick with the routine because they can't imagine what they would do otherwise.

Another result of rigid thinking is the need to do things in the same order even if it wouldn't really matter if they were done in a different order. When Jack was younger we would sometimes go to Legoland as a family. Jack would always want to go on the same rides in the same order, have the same sandwiches for lunch and eat them in the same place as usual. It's as if, were any one thing to be changed, the whole day would become completely unpredictable, and anything might happen. Lots of children with an ASD often have a strong need to keep things the same. They like to always take the same route to a particular place, or they expect to do the same things every time they visit their grandparents, or they expect to go swimming every Saturday morning, without fail. If changes are made they may get quite upset. This is more easy to understand when it's remembered that they have much less ability to think flexibly and imagine a variety of possibilities. A neurotypical child might be disappointed or annoyed at not going swimming, but they can easily think of other things to do. A child with AS might need help to think up alternatives.

Another source of rigid behaviour can be our very literal understanding of language. Most people understand that plans can be made, but they may have to be changed because of unforeseen circumstances. A family may plan to go to the park on Saturday, but if on Saturday morning it's pouring with rain, they might have to rethink this. Some children with an ASD would find the change of plan very disconcerting, even if they realised that the rain would spoil the outing. Because they had been told they would be going to the park, they think they *must* be going to the park. It can help just to use language more precisely. For example, say, 'On Saturday we will go to the park unless it is raining or there is some other problem.' This might seem pedantic but at least it covers all the bases.

We often use language quite loosely. For example, we might say, 'We'll go shopping at about 10,' when that could mean some time between 9.45 and 10.15. Or it could be even later if the phone rings while we're getting ready or we realise we need to put a load of washing in the machine before we go. Again, the person with AS may get very stressed if they are standing at the door ready at 10, because 'You *said* we were going at 10.' This isn't because they are being controlling and unreasonable, it's just that they thought they knew exactly what was going to happen, and now they don't. Problems with plans and timing can be compounded by the fact that some timings have to be relatively precise, while others are more approximate. For example, the precise timing of lessons in secondary school is important. A child would be in big trouble if they turned up for a lesson 15 minutes late. It's important for people to be on time for appointments with the doctor or dentist but, confusingly for an aspie, it's okay for the dentist or doctor to keep you waiting. Someone with AS, particularly a child, may find it difficult to appreciate that some timings matter and some don't.

Why do we have such unusually rigid behaviours?

It comes down to a need to know what is going to happen. If we always do things the same way, if we stick to our rituals and routines, we can anticipate the way things will unfold. Life tends to be more unpredictable for aspies. We often miss the subtle cues that give neurotypicals extra information. Even spoken words cannot always be relied upon because people do not always say what they mean and mean what they say. We are also less able to control what will happen because we are not necessarily good at putting our views across. So it matters to us that some things, at least, are predictable. We have an accurate mental picture of what is going to happen, because that is the way it happened before; we know what to expect. We also find it hard to envisage alternatives, so if one plan is cancelled we may have no idea what might happen instead.

Imagine you book a flight and plan your whole holiday around it. When you turn up at the airport and check in nice and early, you're told by the airline that although your flight is scheduled to depart midday Friday, it's been cancelled. There might be another flight later, or perhaps not until tomorrow. I'd expect you would be a bit annoyed by that, wouldn't you? This is a bit like how we feel about seemingly minor deviations from an expected plan. While you'd be more outraged about your holiday being cut short, we might be more outraged that what was meant to happen, didn't happen. I hope you can see the difference.

Having rituals and rigidities isn't just an aspie trait, we all have them to some extent. For example, do you always *have* to watch the *EastEnders*? Do you have to have a newspaper to read on the train to work, or a cup of coffee first thing in the morning? Do you get a bit stressed and annoyed if your routine is upset? Having a habitual way of doing things frees up our minds to concentrate on other things, or gives us a chance to relax and not need to think at all.

Are rituals good? Most rituals help us feel calm. They make us feel safe and secure in the knowledge that we know what will happen. So if your aspie child has their own particular way of doing things, and it's not causing any problems, it's best to leave well alone. However, if the rituals and need for sameness are beginning to control family life, or if they are marking your child out as a target for bullying (remember how I walked around the playground on hot summer days in an anorak with the hood up?) it may be necessary to intervene.

So should we stop them? All aspie behaviour serves a purpose, and so you need to be careful about trying to stop a particular behaviour. However, we are adaptable creatures (although you may not think it!) and after a while, we can usually find an alternative routine or ritual that serves the same purpose. So if you stop one ritual, it may be horrible for your child, and they may kick up a storm. But after a while, they will probably find an alternative ritual which gives them the same sense of security they need. Or maybe they might find they don't actually need to replace that particular ritual and can manage without it. But stopping a ritual abruptly may be unnecessarily harsh. It's much better to look at how these rituals can be slowly changed. While this may not be pleasant, it will feel much safer for us.

Things that can help with rituals and rigidity

So how do we change them? It's best to change things a little bit at a time. So, for example, with the anorak issue (wearing an anorak in the playground with the hood zipped up even in hot weather), you could swap the anorak for a cagoule when the weather gets hotter. Once the child is used to that, change it for a jacket without a hood. Choose a day when there is something good happening at school, or a day when your child is in a good mood and things are going well. However, you do need to judge just how important a particular ritual is to your child, and whether they are going to panic about even minor changes. You may also find you have to now deal with the difficulty that the ritual was covering up. The child may now find break times more difficult. They may need help to find new, preferably more constructive, strategies to solve the problem of not knowing what to do and feeling awkward. If you have removed that ritual, it is your responsibility to deal with the void it leaves, and the problems that it solved for your child.

It also helps to try and vary things a bit before they become too engrained. For example, if you always go swimming on a Saturday, make a deliberate plan to do something else instead, occasionally. Make sure you give your child plenty of forewarning and make the plan quite concrete. For example, you could say, 'The Saturday after next we will go shopping. You can have £5 to spend and we will visit that shop you like. You can buy something with the money. We won't go swimming because we will be going shopping.'

The importance of using precise language has already been discussed. Sometimes it helps to actually write things down, so they can be referred to when your child needs to check exactly what is going to happen. When Jack is anxious about a change in his routine, he tends to ask the same questions over and over again: 'Where will we be going? What time will we go? What time will we come back?' If we write things down we don't have to keep repeating the same answers, and Jack can reassure himself by looking at the writing. When you are using precise language don't feel you have to be definite about things you cannot know beforehand. For example, it's much better to say, 'We don't know what time we will come home afterwards. Probably some time between 5 and 6.30,' than to say you will all come home at 5.30 and then feel pressured to keep to that time no matter what happens.

It's inevitable that sometimes things will go wrong and your child will get very stressed because their routine or ritual has been disrupted, or because things didn't happen the way that was planned. Here, perhaps the important thing is to respect that although the disruption might seem trivial to you, it's really important to your child. Calming strategies like reassurance, comforting and distraction may be needed. On the other hand, in the long term it may be helpful for your child to realise that though the change is distressing, in the end nothing really bad happened as a result. It's important that the whole family's needs are also respected, and adaptability and the ability to compromise are useful skills to learn.

Changes in routine are inevitable at some point. I find getting new schedules and timetables at university very stressful. My whole routine is going to change and I am constantly wondering about how it is all going to work, and how I am going to cope with it. Everybody finds it a bit difficult but, because of my ASD traits, I find it worries me a lot. And so I have developed strategies to help with this. I look at my new timetable as far in advance as possible to get a rough idea of what it is going to be like. This gives me plenty of time to familiarise myself with the new schedule. I then walk around St Andrews to give myself an idea of the route I will take from lecture to lecture. Sometimes I go in to the lecture theatres and think about where I will sit. This way I feel I really know what is going to happen and how it will work. Finally, I always do something relaxing before I start the new schedule, such as watching some DVDs, or chatting to some friends. This means when I start it I am feeling relaxed, refreshed, and ready to take on my timetable with as few hitches as possible.

Stimming, obsessions and rituals are some of the most obvious behavioural characteristics of people with Asperger syndrome. What is more, they are some of the strongest. If possible, it is best to work with them. In the case of obsessions, they can be used as a driving force for learning and exploration. Stimming and rituals are sometimes needed simply to relieve pressure. When working with them, it's best to aim to gradually modify them, rather than changing them abruptly. Forward planning, gradual desensitisation and general stress relief often play key roles in introducing new situations and scenarios to aspies, and can make the transition much easier.

5

FRIENDSHIPS AND SOCIAL SITUATIONS

Your Heaven, Our Hell

Does Asperger syndrome mean we can't make friends? Often, when parents are told their child has AS, they ask what the diagnosis means. When they are told that the problems include social difficulties, they assume this means their child might not be able to develop friendships. This is simply not true. Friendships are perfectly possible with Asperger syndrome. In this chapter, I will look at why friendships are important, my 'friendship history', how friendships progress, problems people have starting friendships, what can be done to help maintain friendships, and communication.

ARE FRIENDSHIPS IMPORTANT?

The answer to whether friendships are important is a resounding *Yes*. The fact is we are social animals. We have always lived in groups. Even when we were living in caves, we would always stick together. One caveman on his own would not have survived very long. Of course, we also occasionally bashed each other over the head with a mammoth bone, but it was all in good fun. Even nowadays, the human race is very social. With the advent of the internet, we can talk to people on the other side of the world at the click of a button. Just look in your address book – how many people's phone numbers do you have? How many people are you going to see over the next week socially or at work?

People with Asperger syndrome are still human, and so we still want friends. It is just that we may not need as many friends, or need to see them as often as most people do. I sometimes use the analogy of a 'social camel'. We can go for a long time, quite happily, without any social contact, just as a camel can go for a long time without water. However, we will always need some social contact in the end, just as a camel will need to refill with water. How do I know this? When I was signed off school by my psychiatrist, and studying from home, I spent most of my time in my room. For the first few months, I was fine. I didn't need or want any social contact with the outside world. However, as time went on, I would come out of my room more in order to spend some time with my family. After a while, even that wasn't enough. I just got this strong urge to see people. I had to get out of the house to see some different people, and have some different conversations. I needed to refuel with social contact. I had probably lasted a few months without socialising. Other aspies may want more social contact or they may want even less social contact. But sooner or later everyone needs a few other people.

Friendships are also important as a part of growing up. At school, besides all the academic learning, we learn to get on with other people. Within the family people are often very tolerant of our strange quirks and funny little ways. At school we get to try out who we are in the big wide world. We discover which of our traits works well and enables us to get along with other people, and which traits annoy other people or put them off. Knowing how to make friends and how to maintain friendships are very useful life skills. With experience we learn how to negotiate, how to handle conflict and how to get what we want, at least some of the time. As adults we inevitably have to deal with other people, whether this be at work or in the everyday running of our lives. Early friendships prepare us for this.

MY HISTORY WITH FRIENDSHIPS

My first real contact with 'friends' was when I was being home schooled around the age of five. There was a home schooling club every Tuesday afternoon which my mother took me to. We would do things like putting on little plays, arts and crafts, and outdoor activities. However, to be honest, I hated it. I didn't see the point in it, I didn't feel the need to make friends and I just wanted to go home. However, when I started to attend primary school, I was rather scared and felt very alone. At that point, getting a friend became quite important to me. I felt that if I had a friend there, I would make me feel less isolated and vulnerable. I would look less conspicuous and more accepted. The school had a 'buddy' system, whereby I was given a 'buddy' who would show me around and be friends with me. The idea was that after a while I would get drawn into his social circle and make more friends. However, it didn't work. While I was drawn in, it was as the butt of jokes. This just served to make me feel even more insecure and scared, and consequently, I became a social outcast.

I got to a stage where I would just rather be by myself. I just wanted to sit in the library and read rather than feel at a loss in the playground. However, this wasn't allowed. I remember I was really pleased when I broke my arm when horse riding, because then I was told I had to stay in the library instead of going out! When I was forced to go out, I would often just walk along the different coloured lines on the playground. It wasn't exactly fun, but it gave me something to do rather than hanging around on the edge of the playground feeling foolish and friendless. I would also wear a very thick coat. I would always wear it when I went out on break, and it would always be zipped up, with the hood over my head so much you could just see my eyes and nose. While this worked well in winter, in the summer I often felt a bit faint because I was far too hot. However, I would always insist on wearing it because it made me feel safe. It was like a protective barrier between me and the world. At that time I still wanted someone to talk to, to play with, but every time I tried, I just ended up feeling worse, and so I figured it was best not to try.

I think groups of kids often quite like to have someone who is the outcast. That way they can feel superior and avoid the danger of becoming the outcast themselves. They can join together in mutual scorn for the one who doesn't fit in. And the worse thing about it is that the more they reject a particular person, the more different that person's behaviour becomes. The person starts to be defensive and to avoid other people. The person has to find their own ways of dealing with difficult situations, as I did by walking along the lines in the playground. This eccentric behaviour just proves to the others that the person is a weirdo who is not worthy of acceptance. This kind of dynamic can be very difficult to turn around.

Things became worse at secondary school. Here we weren't allowed to wear a coat over our blazers. This made me feel very exposed and insecure. However, I figured it was a fresh start, and that people here would be more adult, and so I tried to make some friends, but this resulted in bullying. Yet again I became the weird kid who walked around looking scared. I was an easy target for anyone who wanted to get a cheap laugh or who wanted to vent their frustration. These experiences would last years, and it wasn't until I got to university that I finally got over these fears and felt able to make a real effort to get to know people.

But there was one place I was accepted. I had carried on with horse riding, and my instructor suggested that I lend a hand at the stables. It was hard graft. I would work from 9 until 5.30 on Saturdays mucking out stables and grooming the horses. I would come back home shattered, but I felt I was contributing, and the ordeal at school would fade from my mind while I was occupied and busy. Most importantly, there I was accepted. I wouldn't say I was making many friends there, but I was accepted. They didn't mind that I was a bit odd, and as long as I could do the work, they were perfectly happy to have me. For four years, this was my only form of social contact that wasn't negative.

It also led to me making one particular friend who has stayed with me for a long time. Early on when I was working at the stables, I met a girl who rode most Saturdays, and usually came up a bit early to help out. We would sometimes talk, or play jokes on each other. But I didn't really get to know Mel until one day I happened to take my camera in to get some photos of the horse I rode. She asked me to take some photos of her horse too and to send them to her, which I did. She then used my email to add me on msn, and since then we have been in communication, usually over the internet. Now we don't see each other often, and we are very different people. She is very outgoing, adventurous and social. Pretty much everything I am not. However, we still talk through msn, and that gives us a channel for more meaningful contact. I will discuss using the internet as a tool for friendships later in the chapter.

For years, Mel was really my only friend. It wasn't until I got to university that I started to branch out more. The university has its own buddying system when senior students become 'academic parents' to first year students. I was very lucky because Hatty, my 'academic mum', knew my family through a distant connection. She also knew about autistic spectrum disorders. When I arrived, she went through the list of all the events that were happening during Freshers' Week with me. She told me which events I would like and which I wouldn't. She also got me into the Ents Crew, who do all the lighting and sound for the bops at the university. Here I met my 'academic dad', Phil, and made many friends. As with my work at the stables, I found being involved in a team working towards a goal was a good environment for making friends. I could not do 'pure socialising' – socialising for the sake of socialising, for example by going to a bar, or a party (which I call primary socialisation). However, socialising as a by-product of an activity I found not only to be possible, but also enjoyable (which I call secondary socialisation). Team-building activities can be a useful way of drawing young people with Asperger syndrome into friendships. It works particularly well if they are able to use one of their skills, or learn a skill, because that way they can make a contribution that the rest of the team really appreciates. Even if they don't have a particular skill, the willingness to regularly put in some graft always earns some respect.

HOW FRIENDSHIPS PROGRESS

It is important to understand that how friendships progress is linked to our developmental age. When children first go to school, it is easy to make friends. Often, children will say that James is my friend because he plays with me. Shared recreational activity is the only necessary component. Here there is not necessarily much social contact, and the games and social rules are quite simplistic. This can be hard for AS and high-functioning autism as while the social rules might be more simplistic, they can still be hard to grasp for young people with AS or high-functioning autism. It is equally hard to initiate this social contact.

Later on, friendships become based on sharing. If James lets me borrow his colouring pencils, he is my friend (or sometimes, if he does not share, he isn't my friend). Here the social rules become more complex, there is a temporary transference of property, and with that comes responsibility. There is much more scope for the friendship to go awry (breaking the pencils). This can result in a need for conflict resolution skills, which we may lack.

In the early teenage and 'tweenager' years, this progresses to sharing interests – such as football, cars, etc. This can be a good way for someone with AS or high-functioning autism to break in, if we have a specialist subject in this area. However, it does rely on the previous two stages being accomplished first.

Finally, in teenage years, friendships become related to talking about feelings, thoughts and beliefs. There is much more rhetoric, which can be hard for us, because of our communication difficulties. Equally, there is much greater complexity on the interaction – is something appropriate to talk about? Who should I share this information with?

The rough age ranges here are for neurotypicals, but this is not to say that people with AS or high-functioning autism will progress at the same rate. It is quite common for our social interaction level to be a few years behind, which makes interaction with our peers harder, when they are all at a much more advanced level. Equally, the complexity of the social interactions and the demands on someone on the spectrum increase – there is much more to think about, and much more scope for a social faux pas.

STARTING FRIENDSHIPS

What prevents children with Asperger syndrome from starting friendships? Well, first of all, sometimes with the best will in the world, parents can in fact prove to be a barrier to friendships. This is not because they try to prevent friendships, but because they try too hard to promote them. Aspies are, unfortunately, rather like mules – if you try and push us to do anything, no matter what it is, we will stick our heels in and refuse to budge. This applies to everything, not only friendships. By all means, encourage us to make friends, but ultimately, if you push us to make friends, we will just become resentful. Essentially, we need to feel in control, because so much that happens to us is beyond our control. I don't want any parents to feel that they have done anything bad by pushing their child to make friends. It is what caring parents would do in this situation. But I believe that the best way is just to encourage, rather than push.

So what does this look like in practice? If your child seems to be getting on well with another child at school, you could suggest doing something together on neutral ground. Your child may have seen the other child at school, but that is a very different environment from home. Equally, home may well be a safe place, and so your child may not feel comfortable having someone from school invade that space. Plan an outing that your child would enjoy, perhaps on a weekend, and ask if they would like to invite a friend to come too. If it's on the weekend your child won't be tired, and if it's an outing that both your child and the friend would enjoy, they don't have to worry about what to do.

If your child is willing, you could have a friend to just play at your house. It may be best to have some ideas ready in case things start to flag. If they are both just hanging around looking awkward they clearly need some help. Also if one child is happily occupied while the other is at a loss, again, they need a bit of direction. You might suggest they could help you make pizzas or cakes for tea, or you could get out some games to play with them. If all else fails, a DVD that they both like can save the day. They may not be socialising if they are watching a DVD but at least they can relax and spend the time enjoyably.

Children with Asperger syndrome often make friends more easily if they share an interest. If they have an interest that will be popular at school, it is worth a little extra encouragement. For example, there is often a cartoon series that lots of children are watching, and related figures and cards they are collecting. If your child gets involved, it gives them something to talk about with other children. The only downside to this is that if the children like to trade collectable cards, it can lead to some tricky situations. For example, if your child's collection is very important to them, it may not be a good idea to take the collection into school, where a highly prized card might go missing.

Older children and teenagers often have developed a special interest (or obsession) and sometimes this interest can be pursued with fellow enthusiasts. For example, some are keen on table-top war games such as Warhammer 40,000, and they meet up at games workshops to buy figures, paint them, and enact battles. Sometimes there are clubs for people who have a special interest, and these may work well for someone with AS because the socialising is a by-product of the shared interest rather than the primary purpose. Also the aspie's knowledge and enthusiasm are respected and welcomed. Usually these kind of interest groups have a mixture of ages, which, again, can work well as there is more of an acceptance of variety and difference. Involvement in a particular project can also be helpful. As I mentioned earlier, I found it much easier to make friends when I got involved with the Ents Crew at university. Everyone is working together towards a particular goal, and often you are accepted and appreciated just because of your willingness to join in, work hard and be committed.

So what hurdles are there when starting a friendship? Well, the biggest is fear of rejection. Remember when I talked about how hard it was to go up and talk to people at primary school – how hard it was just to try and make friends? It was because I had already tried and been rejected. The experiences of rejection lower your self-esteem, which makes it harder to go and try again, and also means when you do try again, because you don't come off so well, you often get rejected again. A downward spiral can develop. So coming up with ways of dealing with rejection is important.

For me, I find it's best to leave it for a while, and try again when you are feeling better.

Another aspect is who you should be friends with. This is a tricky area because some aspies are vulnerable to exploitation. There are a few predators around who will notice a naive, trusting nature and then will persuade that aspie to do whatever they want, 'because we're friends, aren't we?' However, it's not uncommon for aspies to find close friends in surprising places, probably because we don't have a set idea of who should and shouldn't be a friend. Jack used to walk to the local shops and there was a very scruffy cat he would often meet on route, that he always made a fuss of. The owner would sometimes see Jack and chat briefly to him. I'm not sure Jack would have classed the owner as a friend (though he probably classed the cat as a friend), but he liked having someone who recognised him and exchanged a few words with him. Equally contact methods can be unconventional. Look at me and Mel, my friend from horse riding. We meet at most twice a year, and yet we spend ages talking online. For us it is the best way to communicate.

MAINTAINING FRIENDSHIPS

People with AS often need a bit of extra help in keeping good relationships with other people. We often don't know instinctively how to react to the normal stresses and strains of everyday interaction. We are sometimes either too sure that we are in the right and the other person must be at fault, or we are convinced that the other person must be right and in any case we have to give in to keep the friendship of the other person. Jack will do anything his friend tells him to do, rather than risk annoying them. Jordan is much more aware than Jack, but still finds it tricky to know how to assert himself when necessary. There are also quite a few people with AS who will get angry with a friend just because they don't happen to agree with their friend on some issue.

To an extent everyone has these difficulties. No one gets it right all the time, and people learn from their mistakes. If one type of attitude doesn't work, they try another attitude next time.

People can vary their approach, depending on the kind of person they are dealing with, or whether the other person might be in a bad mood, or how important an issue is to them personally. People can also be influenced by what the other person has to say, and change their mind. This kind of flexibility and openness is difficult for people with AS.

For example, you might want to go bowling rather than going to the cinema, but if your friend says the film has really good reviews, and tells you it's just the kind of film you would really enjoy, you might change your mind. But if your friend keeps wanting to go to the cinema you might try to convince them that bowling is good fun. You might also tell them that you haven't had your choice for a while, and this time your choice is to go bowling.

People with AS find all this tricky because we have to be flexible, we have to 'read' the particular social situation, and we have to have some idea of the other person's perspective. We also have to say what needs to be said in the right way. Saying 'Tough luck, mate, we're going bowling!' might be an accurate and fair statement, but it's unlikely to persuade a friend to cooperate. If there was a set of rules we could follow to know how to maintain friendships, we would probably stick to them rigidly, but real life is much too variable and complex.

Children and friendship issues

Something that can help children with AS is to discuss any friendship situations that are causing them a problem. The idea is to help your child understand both their own perspective, and that of the other person. For example, Jordan came home from school one day and was upset because at break time his group of friends always do the game one particular boy chooses, even if Jordan has suggested a really good game. When I asked him how he felt about that, he said he felt sad because none of his friends really like him. If they did like him they would want to do his game. Or they must think his games are really rubbish. I asked him if he thought perhaps his friends just didn't want to annoy the boy who always gets his own way. Maybe Jordan's games were really good, and his friends really do like him, it's just that they are worried about offending the bossy boy. The problem wasn't solved, but Jordan could see that there was a different explanation, which didn't leave him feeling as if he had no friends and no good ideas. Sometimes children with AS don't realise it's possible to see a situation in more than one way.

Suppose your son comes home really angry at his friend saying, 'I hate him, he's not my friend any more!' When you ask him about this, he says his friend is an idiot because he said *Star Trek* (or whatever your son's favourite TV programme is) is rubbish. Later on when he has calmed down you could ask him about the favourite TV programmes of different people in the family. For example, you could ask him what he thinks your favourite TV programme might be, his little brother's favourite TV programme, and so on. Does he think his grandad would enjoy watching his mum's favourite TV programme, or vice versa? You could ask him whether maybe different people like different programmes. It's important not to tell him what to think, but to ask him what he does think. The idea is to help him to come to the realisation that different people can like different things.

Then he might say, 'But he said only stupid losers like *Star Trek*.' You could ask him how he felt at the time (probably angry) and ask what he thought his friend was feeling (probably angry or annoyed). You could then ask him if they had both got angry and just said things because they were angry. You could then say something like, 'Friends sometimes have arguments and shout at each other, but if your friend is usually a good friend, do you think it might be best to try and stay friends, even if he doesn't understand how good *Star Trek* is? Or do you think you don't want him as a friend, even though he's been a good friend, just because of the *Star Trek* issue?'

The important thing in all of this is to begin to enable the person to think about what was happening in a situation, and to see it from another perspective. Children with AS vary in their ability to do this. For example, Jack wouldn't be able to do this, and some children have no patience with it and just dismiss it.

It's always important to ask your child what *they* think about a problem, and to genuinely listen to the answers. This ability to take a step back and take a calm look at things is really useful throughout life.

Another method of working on a friendship issue with your child is to make a cartoon strip of the situation. For example, suppose James is in the playground and can see Matthew playing with a football. James wants to play with Matthew. He picks up the ball and runs off with it. He thinks Matthew will chase him and it will be fun. But Matthew is angry and tells the teacher. If you draw a cartoon strip of this, you can use thought bubbles to show what each person is thinking. For example:

1. Simple picture of James watching Matthew playing with the ball. A thought bubble above his head says, 'I want to play with Matthew.'

2. James runs off with the ball. His thought bubble says, 'Matthew can play chase with me.' Matthew's thought bubble says, 'Hey! He stole my ball!'

3. Matthew tells the teacher. He is pictured saying, 'James stole my ball!'

4. The teacher talks to James. She says, 'You mustn't steal other people's things.' James' thought bubble says, 'I didn't steal his ball! I wanted to play chase.'

This shows the different perspectives very clearly. It shows why James thought he was starting a fun game of chase which Matthew would enjoy, and it shows why Matthew thought James had stolen his ball. You can use very simple stick figures, so the cartoon strips can be drawn very quickly. You could also do another cartoon strip showing what to do next time. James approaches Matthew and asks, 'Do you want to play chase?' Matthew says either 'Okay' or 'No thanks.'

The advantage of using cartoon strips is that they are visual and avoid the problems of trying to just explain things verbally. A cartoon like this shows what happened and why it happened. Many people with AS find it easier to make sense of something they can see than something they have to listen to, and it can be looked at as often as necessary. Importantly, they also show thoughts: we lack the ability to pick up on subtle nonverbal cues that you use to tell how someone is feeling, or what they are thinking. Using thought bubbles can help us to develop the ability to predict how someone might think or feel.

Teenagers and adults: meeting new people

Before we even get to the point of making friends, it's important to have some idea of what to say when meeting new people, particularly in social gatherings where meeting new people is the main purpose of the event. When I met someone new, I used to have a basic set of things to say. I would say, 'Hi, how are you?', and I would ask them what they did, and this would usually lead the other person to ask how I was and what I did. After that I was out of ideas, so I would be very British and talk about the weather. After that, I would be completely stumped. I didn't know what else I could talk about. Why? Because I didn't understand the social rules which dictated what was acceptable conversation and what was not.

It's good to ask people questions about themselves but these have to be the right kind of questions. 'Whereabouts do you live?' is fine, but 'How old are you?' and 'What's your favourite colour?' are not. It's good to talk about general subjects such as current affairs and music, but not good to express strong opinions. If the other person asks a question, such as 'How did you get here today?', it's not good to go into too much detail ('I turned left when I came out of my road, then I walked up the hill past the supermarket, then…') but it's also not helpful to just give a minimal answer, such as 'I walked.' I was so worried about getting it wrong, I just went with things that I knew were acceptable. I didn't dare try out anything new. Gradually I learned to try new topics of conversation, and to pace my questions and answers so that we both contributed to the conversation equally, but this took time and practice.

One particular problem that we have is a tendency to talk too much about our specialist subject. I have met so many aspies, who have talked about train timetables or whatever their current obsession is at great length, before I got a chance to break into the conversation. And I know I am bad at remembering that not everyone is as interested in psychology as I am. So I try to limit myself to a maximum of two minutes of talking about it before pausing for breath and giving the other person a chance to speak.

COMMUNICATION

One key area where we often have problems is in understanding what people are really trying to communicate to us. In the first chapter I talked about how things like subtext, facial expressions, body language and social cues can be hard for us to pick up on. When it comes to friendships, picking up on these is very important.

For example, subtext. Subtext is a message that is implied by what is said, rather than stated. Suppose a friend says, 'I'm really struggling with this maths. But you're really good at it, aren't you?', the subtext is, 'Will you please help me with this maths?' But aspies may not get that. An aspie might reply, 'Yes, I'm pretty good at it,' and think it's the end of the conversation. The friend might then feel annoyed or hurt because they think you have deliberately ignored their plea for help. Or your girlfriend might say, 'I saw this really nice bracelet in the catalogue. I could show you if you want.' If it's near her birthday, the subtext is probably, 'Please would you buy it for my birthday?' but, again, an aspie might not realise this.

Facial expressions can cause problems too. Knowing when someone is pleased to see you, feeling down or feeling stressed are important skills to have for a friendship. But they are skills that we find hard to acquire. The problem is made worse because we don't tend to make as much eye contact as neurotypicals, and we may not look at their faces much, either. Being able to 'read' someone's face and know when they are feeling down allows you to know how to respond in the right way. You can say, 'You look a bit down. Is something wrong?' and the other person will probably be pleased you have noticed. This awareness can help build the friendship. However, people with Asperger syndrome often don't have this ability and so they may be viewed as being cold or insensitive.

Most of us do care a lot about our friends, because a friendship tends to be quite important to us. We don't make new friends as easily as most people so we want to keep the friendships we have. We just find it hard to know when someone is having problems. People don't normally say, 'I am feeling down, will you help me?'

Body language is something which has always baffled me. For example, I am told that when I am giving one of my talks, it is best to use my hands expressively, face the audience, move around and smile. Personally I don't see why my performance would be any different if I faced the wall with my arms crossed with a big frown on my face. Unfortunately, body language seems to be very important and so it is something I have had to try and learn. But it's difficult for us to recognise that, for example, a slumped posture and shoulders, a slow gait, and looking down are signs of someone feeling low. Body language can also indicate when someone is getting impatient (crossed arms, foot tapping) or bored (yawning, looking at other things) or is in some other state of mind (pleased, worried, excited and so on). This is information that the aspie may miss. It can cause problems because the other person may assume the aspie is just deliberately ignoring the way he feels.

Social cues can be hard for people with AS to pick up. Social cues are things like knowing when it is your turn to speak, when to stop speaking, and noticing when the other person wants to finish the conversation. Most people seem to understand social cues intuitively but we have to learn through trial and error. I have learned some skills, but I still find it hard to know when I can jump in with my bit of the conversation. So when I am with friends, I have had to learn to wait about two seconds before I say anything in order to make sure they have stopped speaking. If I didn't, then it could seem like I was butting in. Unfortunately, my method still means there can be a bit of an unnaturally long silence between people speaking. But waiting two seconds works for me.

Subtext, tone of voice, facial expression, body language and social cues all convey information to most people, but aspies may be much less aware of these subtleties. We rely much more on the words people say, and even then we rely on people actually saying what they mean. Asking friends and family to be direct and clear in what they say can help. I think that people with AS telling friends about Aspergers early on is a good move. Once someone is friends with them, they are likely to be fine about it. Explaining what Aspergers is can be really useful. You will probably find that they will take an interest in what Aspergers is, which again is great, as it will help them to understand why your son or daughter is the way they are. Friends need to understand that aspies may not pick up on body language, facial expressions and tone of voice. This can really help friendships survive.

For example, if I ask a friend, 'How are you?', and she replies, 'I'm fine,' I assume that she is fine. I may not notice that she is saying it in a way that most people know to mean, 'I'm am not fine, talk to me.' Friends need to know that saying what they mean ('I'm feeling down') and what they want ('Please help me') really helps me to respond in the right way. Equally, if I'm doing something that annoys the other person, they need to tell me, rather than just behaving in an irritated way. Many very promising friendships have broken up because of a lack of clarity in communication, so it is really important to get this right from the start.

The 'Do I look fat in this?' scenario

There is a special kind of permutation of social interaction which has always really puzzled me. It is the 'white lie'. Suppose a female friend (not necessarily a girlfriend) sees you, you chat, and after a while she says, 'I bought this dress yesterday. Do you think it makes me look a bit fat?' This is, in my opinion, a question all men should be trained to respond to, in order to avoid the fire storm if they get it wrong. Most men know that the only possible right answer to this question is, 'No, you look great.' However, we aspies are more logical about it. Let's say your friend does look fat in that new dress. Wouldn't she want to know? Wouldn't it help to know which dresses are and are not flattering on her? Aren't we always taught that honesty is the best policy? And so if we answer honestly ('Yes, I think you're right, you do look a bit chunky') we don't understand how we have made a social gaffe. This type of situation requires tact rather than truth and is, in my opinion, one of the hardest bits of social interaction for people with Asperger syndrome to learn.

The problem is partly that we respond to the words and miss the subtext. The words ask a simple question, 'Do I look fat?', and would seem to require a simple yes or no answer. The subtext is, 'I spent money on this dress yesterday because I thought it made me look attractive. But now I'm worried that it actually makes me look unattractively chubby. If that is the case I have wasted my money and I am too fat.' That is a lot of subtext. But the problem is also that we miss the emotional content of the question, which is, 'Please reassure me that the dress looks good so that I don't have to feel bad about wasting my money and being too fat.'

These situations occur surprisingly often. For example, a friend might go to a lot of trouble cooking a nice meal for you and then ask you what you thought of it. He probably doesn't want your advice on how to do it better next time, he wants you to express appreciation. The emotional content is that he wants you to be pleased with the meal because that's why he made the effort of preparing it. Or someone buys you a gift for your birthday, not realising it's something you dislike. She doesn't want an honest appraisal of her gift ('Actually I don't wear aftershave, particularly aftershaves that smell like this. Next time a gift voucher would probably be better'), she wants you to be pleased. Then she will feel glad she went to the trouble of choosing a nice gift for you. Of course the downside to this is that she may now buy you aftershave for Christmas as well.

Another area where tact rather than honesty is sometimes required is in appearing to be interested in a topic of conversation that you actually find quite boring. This seems to be particularly necessary in family gatherings. I may not be interested in all the details about someone's new graphics card or someone's theory on how to overhaul the National Health Service, but if I want to keep a good relationship with them it's necessary to at least pretend that I'm taking it all in. There have probably been times when I've been a bit boring but they've listened to me.

Present giving is also sometimes a bit tricky for people with AS. The problem is that some of us tend to give a present that we ourselves really like, or a present we think the other person needs. So an aspie might buy his mum a football mug if he is keen on football, or a book about slimming or some anti-wrinkle cream, because he can see that those are things she needs. He may not realise that, because she has no interest in football, the football mug will not give her the same pleasure that it would give him. This is a problem with understanding the other person's perspective. The book about slimming and the anti-wrinkle cream may be useful, but they are not tactful presents (unless the person has asked for them). It's like saying, 'I thought about you when choosing my gifts, and I realised you need to lose a bit of weight, and you're getting a bit crinkly, too.'

I find that having someone who can just act as a guide on social interaction really helps. I sometimes come away from a conversation with a friend thinking I've missed something. There was some subtext that I hadn't understood. I recount the conversation to a friend who acts as a social translator, so I know what was really meant. Some people achieve the same thing with a mentor, who can either be the same age or older. However, it can be harder to build the same rapport with someone you are 'set up with' than with someone you already know and trust. I am told that often an older sister is really good at this.

I think that reading can be a great help in understanding social situations, particularly for young teenagers. When we become teenagers, the social rules change a lot. Most people realise it's necessary to throw out some of the social rules that applied when they were children, and to work out new rules. But aspies keep trying to use the old rules and we keep finding they just don't fit. Reading can actually help with this.

A great example of this is the Harry Potter novels. This might seem surprising because the books are all about a boarding school for wizards. However, they also cover a wide range of social situations which are common to older children and teenagers. For example, they deal with the problems of starting a new school, bullying, being misunderstood, having arguments with friends, right through to boyfriend or girlfriend situations and exams. While I will admit that some, if not most, of the situations are rather unlikely to occur in real life, the underlying social element can be really useful. The narrative format of the books enables you to learn what the protagonist is thinking and feeling in these situations. This can be useful helping yourself to identify what you are thinking and feeling in situations in your own life.

Another advantage of using novels in understanding social situations is that you can go back and read them over and over again. You can do the same with films: here you lose the ability to read someone's thoughts, but gain a better insight into body language and facial expressions. The ideal is to read the book and watch the film. That way you can see how the emotional processes described in the book are portrayed by the actors. This can help you to have a better understanding of facial expressions and body language in real life. Teachers and parents are often a good source of advice when choosing the right book or film.

Role-playing can be very useful. If you know that you are going to be in a difficult social situation, you can try rehearsing it with a supportive friend or family member. People often do this in preparation for job interviews, but it can also be used in much more informal contexts. For example, if a friend is unintentionally annoying you by always phoning at a bad time, you can work out what to say when he does this. You can practise with someone you trust, who might also give you advice on the kind of thing to say and the way to say it.

One of the ways for aspies to communicate with friends is on the internet. Here, you don't have to worry about tone of voice, facial expressions or body language because only words are used. Conversation is slowed right down, because each person has to type out their words, press send, and then wait for a reply.

Emoticons can also be used, such as :(which is a sad face if you look at it sideways :) which means happy or :P which is a tongue sticking out. On the internet people use these to supplement the words. For example, 'I got 70 per cent in my Maths exam' might be happy or sad, depending on how well you expected to do. Email can also be useful, if a bit more cumbersome. When I'm at home I have even been known to email my dad, who is just downstairs, to ask him what's for lunch!

Finally, if all else fails, life itself tends to ensure we improve our ability to make and keep friends. We learn a lot by experience, by watching others and by trial and error (mostly error!). What I have suggested are, I hope, ways of increasing the success rate of trial and error. But when it comes down to it, I learned simply by watching the other kids in the playground and trying to imitate them. Sometimes simply encouraging or aiding this can be the best solution.

6

SHOPPING, TRAVELLING AND HOLIDAYS

Out and About in a Scary World

In this chapter I'm going to cover everyday activities such as shopping and budgeting, and travelling on public transport. I'm also going to talk about less frequent but important activities, such as going on holiday. People with Asperger syndrome vary a lot in their abilities, and sometimes even the most able and academically clever have a problem with some everyday tasks. Some aspies will manage shopping or travelling by bus easily, some will find them more tricky. They need a bit of guidance and preparation in order to have the confidence to do these things on their own.

Often children with AS are less clear about what to expect when, for example, going to buy something on their own for the first time. This makes them unsure about what to do. Children without AS seem to know that when you go shopping, you choose the thing you want, take it to the till and pay for it, the cashier puts the item in a bag, and gives it to you. They have seen their mum doing this many times and this is all they need in order to form a pretty accurate idea of what to do when they try buying something on their own. This is called a procedural schema – a mental template of what to do. Aspies don't seem to pick up this kind of knowledge quite as easily.

To build up a schema requires a good understanding of things like intentions, which requires theory of mind, something people with AS sometimes have problems with. It also requires the person to attend to what is happening. However, people with AS may well not find that what someone is doing is very worthy of attention. Aspies may much prefer to look at the LED screen on the till, or the patterns on the counter top, etc. This can mean we fail to build up accurate schemas.

Sometimes the person with AS knows what to expect (i.e. has a schema), and has successfully shopped or travelled alone many times. Then the unexpected happens. The bus just doesn't arrive at the bus stop, or the train home is cancelled. The aspie may panic because they don't know what to do. The schema (the mental plan) has deviated from the norm – there is no longer a set script for what to do! This can result in the aspie losing confidence and refusing to catch the bus any more, or refusing to ever go into town by train again in case the return train is cancelled. We aspies are often less good at improvising solutions when we are under pressure, and find it particularly difficult to explain ourselves to strangers if necessary. We do not find it easy to extrapolate from our schema, or adapt another one. For example, if we need to ask someone at the station when the next train is, or if we have to ask for a particular item in a shop, this can be quite daunting, particularly for younger aspies. Some may not even think that asking is an option – it was not in their original schema. Or they may try and apply the schema anyway, and deliberately get on the next train to arrive, even though it is the wrong one. We are not good at flexible thinking and can be at a loss if things don't happen the way they should do. For this reason it's often necessary to pre-plan what to do if something goes wrong (I call this a catastrophe and contingency plan). This acts as a kind of safety net.

Related to this is a difficulty with generalising knowledge and adapting it. Even if an aspie has learned to do one particular train journey, they may be nervous about trying another route in case there are unexpected differences that they might have difficulty with. Here, the aspie has learned the schema for one particular route (or can even specify a particular train departure) but, unlike neurotypicals, they cannot generalise it to all trains. They learn the journeys completely independently, in the same way you would learn getting a train and taking a plane independently, rather than learn a general 'train schema'. For a long time my brother Jack would only shop at the local newsagent. He'd been there many times and knew what to expect. Then that shop closed and he had to go to a small supermarket attached to a petrol station. The problem was that the till staff would automatically ask each customer, 'Any fuel?' because they needed to know if the customer was also paying for filling up their car. The question didn't even make any sense to Jack and he was at a loss to know what was expected of him. After that he was reluctant to go to that shop, and reluctant to try any other shops either. Often we aspies like to stick with what we know rather than try other shops, or other bus routes, in case the procedure is different and we are put in a situation where we are not sure what to do.

The following sections go into more specific detail about how to make sure the person with AS knows what to do, learns to generalise the knowledge, and knows how to deal with the unexpected. It may be that this is unnecessary for some aspies. But many aspies have a problem with anxiety and their confidence is easily undermined by the routine mishaps of life. Preparation is a way of avoiding some of those mishaps.

PREPARATION

Preparation is about knowing what to expect, and knowing how to deal with the unexpected. The kind of preparation which works will vary depending on the age of the person with AS, their individual strengths and weaknesses, and the way they learn best. Ways of preparing could be role-play, cartoon strips, bullet points, walking through and talking through.

Role-play

Role-play can work well with children with AS. Essentially it is just acting out a scenario such as going into a shop to buy something, or getting on a bus, asking for a ticket, paying for it and sitting down. In many ways this is the kind of pretend play that most children do at a younger age, and it does help prepare them for real life situations. But lots of aspies are not very interested in pretend play at that stage. It's important that your child doesn't feel silly or patronised when trying out role-play, so it helps to try and keep it realistic. Acting out a scenario may only take a minute or two and doesn't have to be very elaborate. It may help to use real money, because your child needs to work out if they have enough money to buy an item, and whether they will receive any change back. One advantage of acting things out is that you can weed out errors that you might not have anticipated. For example, some people with AS may use overly formal language, such as saying, 'Thank you, sir, that's very kind of you, sir,' to the cashier at the end of the transaction.

Cartoon strips

Simple cartoon strips showing what to do when buying something at a shop or using a bus can also be quite useful. You don't have to be good at art. Just use very basic stick figures, speech balloons and thought bubbles. For example, picture one can show the person waiting at a bus stop. Picture two shows him getting on the bus. Picture three shows him asking for a ticket; use a speech balloon and the actual words your child will need to use. Picture four can show the hand giving the money, with writing beneath the picture saying, 'Pay for the ticket.' Picture five shows the hand taking the ticket, with writing underneath saying, 'Take the ticket.' The last drawing shows the person sitting down on the bus. You could also add a couple of drawings showing when to get off the bus.

Cartoons like these can be very helpful for people who are visual learners and for people who need things presented in a very simple way. Their advantage is that the person doing the bus journey can use them for reference when they are actually on the journey. My brother Jack would find a cartoon strip much more easy to understand than verbal instructions. I wouldn't rely on a cartoon strip as the main method of preparation, but it's a really useful supplement.

Bullet points

Bullet points are another useful aid which can be referred to when the person with AS is unsure. For example, if the aspie is doing a train journey on their own for the first time, just make a note of the important points in list form. It would might look something like this:

- Queue for the ticket.
- Ask for a return ticket to London.
- Pay for ticket.
- Put ticket into automatic barrier.
- Take ticket when you've gone through the automatic barrier.
- Go to Platform 5.
- Check destination of next train (look at overhead display on the platform).
- Catch train.
- Get out at Waterloo.
- Put ticket in automatic barrier.
- Take ticket when through barrier, and put in wallet for return journey.

This kind of list is a useful reminder when the person with AS is en route. It may be important to prepare in other ways if this is their first journey on their own, but the list can be reassuring, particularly if the person lacks confidence. It's also very easy to make this kind of list, and if, in the end, the aspie doesn't need to refer to it, you haven't wasted a lot of effort. If, another time, they need to make a different journey, it's easy to make another list with just the new details on it.

Walking through

Walking through involves going with the person with AS when they go shopping or use public transport for the first time, and showing them what to do. Point out the important details, such as what ticket to ask for, and when to get ready to get off the bus. Next time you do it, let your child take charge and just be on hand for support. This is useful because you will see if there are any gaps in your child's knowledge, where they feel unsure of what to do. The next step can be to follow at a distance. If the aspie is taking a bus or train journey on their own, it is possible to follow in the car. This may seem over-the-top, and is probably unnecessary in most cases, but it depends on the age of the person with AS, their abilities and their level of confidence.

Following at a distance can sometimes show up problems which don't come to light until the person with AS is on their own. For example, if your child was learning to go to the local shop and buy something on their own, the first time you would show your child what to do, the second time you would just go with them and let them take charge, and the third time you would follow at a distance. It may only be when following at a distance that you realise that, although your child knows how to cross the road, they may not understand that it's important to choose the right place to cross. Distractions can sometimes be more of a problem when the person with AS is on their own. Jack is very scared of dogs, so if a person with a dog was walking towards him, he might dash across the road without checking properly that it was safe. It also shows up if the aspie has any odd mannerisms which might draw unwelcome attention. Jack sometimes chuckles or makes little comments to himself, and people on a bus or train would notice this if he was on his own, whereas they don't if he is with someone because they assume he is talking to his companion.

Talking through

Talking through is fairly obvious. This is the most simple and easy way to prepare, and is well suited to more able and more mature people with AS. It's useful to ask questions, just to make sure the other person knows what they are doing, and that there are no small gaps in their understanding which might cause a problem.

Once the person with AS is able to do a particular journey by bus without any problem, for example, it's useful to develop this by trying a different journey. There may be small but important details that are different. Perhaps the stop at the beginning or end of the route is a request stop, so the person has to learn the procedure for that. The person needs to know how to work out when they are getting near the new destination, for example by looking out for a particular road or landmark. If you can anticipate these new elements and prepare for them, it avoids the person's growing confidence being undermined by an unforeseen problem. The ideal is to steadily expand the person's skill base, so they become more capable and more independent, and more confident. Even now, despite happily being able to travel the country by public transport to do my talks, if I have a route I am unsure of I still sometimes talk it though with my dad (who usually just nods along).

ALLOWING FOR THE UNEXPECTED

However well people plan and prepare, there will always be situations which couldn't have been anticipated and which can be problematic. For example, trains sometimes get delayed or cancelled, and this can be particularly difficult if you need to be somewhere at a particular time, or if you miss a connecting train because of it. Sometimes the bus is full and it's not possible to get on it, which can be worrying if you are relying on it to get you home. Then there are the errors which most of us make occasionally. It's not difficult to accidentally get on the wrong train and end up miles from where you should be, or to miss your stop on the bus because you were engrossed in a book. The problem for people with AS is that we tend to find it difficult to think quickly and flexibly in order to work out a solution, particularly when we get stressed, which usually happens when things are going wrong. Also we are not good at talking our way out of tricky situations by asking other people for information, or by explaining ourselves.

When I was 12 or so, I went down the road to the corner shop. Mum had asked me to buy a newspaper and some milk, and I could use whatever money was left over to buy myself something. I got the newspaper and milk, and a bar of chocolate for myself, and went to the till. But when the cashier told me the total cost, I realised I hadn't got quite enough money. I was so flustered, I didn't know what to do. Then I started thinking, 'Maybe the cashier thinks I'm trying to cheat him,' and then, 'He might call the police!' In my mind the situation was snowballing to disastrous proportions. Luckily the cashier guessed what the problem was and suggested that if I didn't have enough money I could just buy two things instead. So I left the bar of chocolate and just bought the milk and newspaper. For the next five years, if I went shopping I always carried a calculator with me so I could check that I had enough money with me before going to the till.

There are three things that I think are helpful when dealing with the unexpected: a mobile phone, an autism alert card and a contingency fund, which is an extra five or ten pounds the aspie always has with them, only to be used in an emergency.

Mobile phone

A mobile phone is very helpful when travelling by public transport. I have often needed to make long and complicated journeys by train, and there have been many occasions when I have been stranded on a platform because my connecting train has been cancelled. It's been really useful to be able to phone home because my dad will check on the internet to find out the latest rail information and the best option. Even if the person at the other end of the phone isn't able to access relevant information, they usually give sensible advice. Just knowing that you don't have to completely rely on your own initiative can make the situation less daunting. Also, of course, if I realise I'm going to be late for an appointment I can phone ahead to explain (always make sure you take the relevant phone numbers with you). This takes a lot of the stress out of train delays. It's worth noting that some mobile phones have a facility that enables them to be tracked by GPS. If your child with AS has one of these phones you can track where they are. This way you can make sure that the journey is going according to plan, and if your child gets lost you can work out their location. However, please ask before you do this.

Autism alert card

An autism alert card can be very useful. This is a small card, available from the NAS in the UK, that states, 'This person has autism/Asperger syndrome' and gives a short explanation. It can be used if the person with AS gets into a tricky situation when out and about. When a friend of mine with AS was travelling by train, the ticket inspector told him he actually had the wrong kind of ticket. My friend hadn't realised that his ticket could only be used within certain hours, and not during peak times. He felt quite panicky because he thought he might be prosecuted for trying to defraud British Rail. Because he was so alarmed, it was difficult for him to think clearly and explain himself. It was helpful to be able to show the inspector the card, because he then became more patient and understanding. In the end the situation was easily resolved by paying the excess fare. The value of the card is that it communicates that you have certain difficulties at times when you are a bit panicked and need the other person to be considerate.

Contingency fund

A contingency fund is always useful because having some extra cash will often help solve a problem. If you make a mistake on public transport and end up in the wrong place, some extra money will buy another ticket or, if necessary, a taxi home. If you are charged more than you expected in a shop or cafe, having a spare fiver can be really useful. Having some extra cash is particularly important for children and people who don't have a credit or debit card, because if they run out of money due to unexpected circumstances, they have no easy way of getting more. However, it is very important that the person with AS understands that the money is only for an emergency. If the person spends more than they should because they know they have this extra cash, it won't be there when they genuinely need it. For this reason it's best if the money is kept separately from the normal spending money, or at least in a separate part of the wallet.

SENSORY ISSUES

Sensory issues are often a complicating factor when shopping or travelling on public transport. There is often so much going on that we get sensory overload. In shopping centres there are often crowds of people and lots of shops have music playing in the background. Some shops now have an anti-theft alarm at the exit that seems to go off quite frequently. In supermarkets there are often announcements over the public address system and the tills bleep when they are scanning purchases.

For people with AS all this sensory input is constantly distracting. Our whole system becomes alerted by the jumble of noise and movement, and we have to keep refocusing. For children the problem is worse because they have to follow their parent around and often there is a lot of waiting in queues followed abruptly by rushing to the next shop or rushing back to the car because the parking ticket is running out. In supermarkets they have to be careful not to stand in the way of other people's trolleys, and also deal with their own boredom as they trail around the aisles after their distracted parent.

I think it is worth looking at relaxation techniques, for when the stress becomes too much, for you, or for your child. One that I have found works well is to sit down, with feet flat on the ground, and arms by your sides. Take a steady deep breath in, hold it for a couple of seconds, then slowly breathe out, and keep doing this until you feel calmer. If possible, close your eyes and just concentrate on your breathing, letting go of all other thoughts. Sometimes I have found doing this leaves me feeling a lot more able to cope with problems than before.

There are quite a few sensory issues when travelling by train. Trains can be very noisy, particularly if you have to stand near the section which joins two carriages together. If the train is crowded you often have to stand very close to other people, which gets quite uncomfortable. Sometimes you end up almost pressed up against complete strangers, while trying to avoid all eye contact. It's necessary to keep your balance while the train is in motion, and a sudden jolt can almost pitch you into someone's lap! Travelling on the Underground in the rush hour is possibly one of the worst situations for sensory overload. In the station there is a constant press of people going in all directions, which gets quite dizzying, and then there is the scrum to actually get on the train, and the necessity of having to stand almost chest to chest with all the other commuters. It leaves many aspies longing for some personal space and fresh air.

At the opposite extreme, sitting in a quiet train on a long journey can be almost too relaxing. When I did my regular Friday night commute from Bath back to Guildford, I would always be tired as it would be the end of a long day, and several times I caught myself dozing off. My big fear was that I would fall asleep and fail to get off to catch the connecting train. Then I would end up in the centre of London with an invalid ticket. The invalid ticket might not seem like the most pressing concern in that situation, but, like many aspies, I have a big fear of doing anything wrong. I remember a young man with Aspergers telling me that, when buying a ticket, he had asked for a disabled person's discount, but was actually given a young person's discount. He didn't notice until the ticket inspector on the train asked him for proof that he was entitled to a young person's discount. He was unable to provide this and got so stressed he almost had a meltdown right there on the train.

Some aspies find travelling on a train uncomfortable because the seats are arranged so that you are often facing another person, unlike a bus, where most of the seats face forwards. If you are sitting by the window you can look outside, but if not it can be difficult to know what to look at, as you have to avoid making eye contact. It helps to have a book or a magazine, particularly on a long journey. An iPod or MP3 player with ear pieces can be very useful. The music helps to block out some of the noise, and also relieves some of the stress.

A lot of aspies like to have their own personal space, and this can work well on a quiet train as people do not tend to sit next to strangers unless they have to. If the train is moderately busy it's more likely that someone will take the seat next to you. When I was commuting I would put my (large) rucksack on the seat next to me and stare out of the window. People are reluctant to ask you to move your bag so that they can sit down. However, it would obviously be unfair to block a seat in this way if the train was crowded.

One particular strength people with AS may have when using public transport is a fascination with timetables and routes. An aspie can become a bit of an expert in this area. Others become fans of the different types of trains and buses, and love travelling on them. There are probably a fair proportion of aspies among train spotters. Once the basics of travelling on public transport have been mastered, all sorts of possibilities open up. The ability to get where you want, when you want, without having to depend on other people, grants some welcome independence.

BUDGETING

Although there are some advantages to shopping on the internet, the downside is that it's possible to spend huge amounts of money in just a few minutes. A parent told me that, without her knowledge, her son had memorised her credit card number and used it to buy Pokémon cards on the internet. A week later, when she tried paying for her weekly shop at the supermarket, she discovered her credit card had been maxed out. He thought that, as he hadn't actually taken her card, it wasn't stealing. Incidentally, a lot of younger aspies get confused about credit cards. For example, when my youngest brother wanted to buy something, and was told it cost too much money, he said, 'You don't have to use money, you can use your credit card.'

There is also the problems in anticipating exactly how worthwhile a particular purchase will be. Jack had been saving up the money he had been given for Christmas and his birthday, and had ended up with over a hundred pounds. He searched on the internet and made a detailed list of about 30 he wanted to buy, together with their cost. The problem was that they were all Sonic the Hedgehog cuddly toys of various sizes. He didn't realise that having loads of cuddly Sonics might not be that much better than just having a few, or that he might get more entertainment from buying some DVDs and comic books. Luckily, when we talked to him about this, he changed his mind.

Some aspies are easily taken in by advertisements, and then are disappointed when the product doesn't fulfil its promise. This is because we tend to take things literally. We sometimes don't realise that the claims made in adverts are usually exaggerated. For example, an aspie might buy a particular aftershave because in the ad girls seem to find the smell irresistible. He might then feel quite cheated if girls didn't seem to even notice when he wore it. Jordan thinks that the more you eat a food that is advertised as slimming, the more weight you will lose. So if you eat six pots of diet yoghurt for dessert one day you will lose more weight than if you only ate one. Incidentally, lots of children with AS seem to enjoy memorising the words to TV adverts and parroting them. Overall, aspies must be the advertiser's favourite kind of people!

We sometimes find it hard to keep track of invisible costs. I hear lots of stories of teenagers buying a contract mobile phone, talking and texting and downloading ringtones and then getting a huge bill at the end of the month that they weren't expecting.

So how do we solve money issues? What I have found helpful is to work out a few guidelines. For example, unless I am internet shopping, I always pay in cash to remind me of exactly what the cost really is – often even neurotypicals can get caught by not registering the cost that happens when you stick that credit card into the machine. When I'm deciding whether something is worth buying, I ask myself these questions:

- If it costs under £15 – Do I really want it?

- £15 to £50 – Do I really need it?

- £50 to £100 – Do I really need it? Have I looked for the best price? Have I checked reviews for this product?

- Over £100 – Wait a week and then ask myself the above questions again.

Obviously it's necessary to adjust the amounts of money, relative to the available budget.

Although some of us have problems with money, there are people with AS who are very astute and really enjoy being able to manage their own budget effectively. We can also get very good at this when we have a good set of rules for how to allocate money. Incidentally, there are probably quite a few accountants who have Asperger syndrome.

HOLIDAYS

Holidays are great, aren't they? You get out of your old routine, see new places, stay somewhere new, meet new people – all things that aspies hate about holidays. That's not to say that I have never enjoyed my holidays. It's just that holidays need to be managed in the right way to minimise the pitfalls and to maximise the positives. With some simple adjustments, and some forward planning, holidays can become a lot more enjoyable all round.

When you're planning a holiday, it's a good idea to include your child with AS in the discussions about where to go and what to do. If you find out what would appeal to your child, it's more likely they will do their best to enjoy it when you go. You will also know what to avoid. If you find that your child is strongly against one type of holiday, it's worth asking some questions to find out what the problem is. It may be that they have some kind of misunderstanding about what the holiday involves. For example, when we asked Jordan if he would like a beach holiday, he was definitely against it. But when we asked why he said that it was because it takes a very long time to drive to the beach in the morning, and then at the end of the day it takes an equally long time to drive home again. We had to explain that we would be staying in a house near the beach, so that wouldn't be a problem. Sometimes the obvious isn't so obvious to the person with AS.

When you have decided on where to go, it may help to involve the aspie in choosing the accommodation. Of course it's important to allow your other children (if you have any) the same level of involvement, otherwise they will become resentful. If necessary narrow it down to two or three places to go to before asking for preferences. Seeing pictures of the place where you might stay really helps to give a more realistic idea of what it's like. These pictures are also very useful nearer the time of the holiday, because they make the house or hotel seem familiar before you go.

When the holiday is approaching, it's important to have a discussion about your expectations of what you will do on holiday. Sometimes people with AS cannot really imagine what the holiday will be like. They have no idea in their mind of what might happen, and this can make them quite anxious. It's best to talk through what the new routine might be. For example, if you are staying in a hotel, talk about what time you will go and have breakfast, how you *might* spend the morning, what you will do for lunch, and so on. Make sure you don't word things too definitely, though. It's better to say, 'We'll go and have breakfast sometime between about 8 and 9.30. Then *maybe* we'll go to the beach, or we might explore the town.' Otherwise any deviation from what you have said might cause problems ('But you *said* we would have breakfast at 8.30!'). Look at pictures again of the place where you will stay and of the locality. It all helps to give the aspie a realistic idea of what to expect.

Long, tedious journeys tend to be a feature of travelling to a holiday destination. Travelling by plane can have both positives and negatives for children with AS. Flying typically involves a lot of waiting around at the airport, and then sitting in a confined space with lots of strangers on the plane. This means there is a lot of opportunity for children to get bored and fractious in a very public way. On the other hand many aspies are fascinated by the logistical process, engineering, people or technology used in planes and airports.

It's a good idea to aim to arrive at the airport with plenty of time to spare. This does extend the amount of time to fill, but at least this way you allow for the unexpected en route, such as traffic jams. Having to rush around frantically almost guarantees that an aspie child will become difficult. Equally, they will pick up on your anxiousness about missing your check-in, and amplify it in themselves. Find a good place to sit where you can watch the planes. When I am waiting to fly home from Edinburgh airport I have a nice little spot where I sit and just watch planes land, taxi, refuel and take off. It really is fascinating.

The wait at the airport can also be used to explain what is going to happen. For example, you can talk about going through security, getting on the aircraft, taking your seats and so on. In many ways talking about this at the airport is the ideal time, because you can actually point things out. For example, some airports have a video of the security procedure on constant replay so that everyone knows what will happen. However, it is also worth doing this well beforehand (i.e. when booking, a week before, and the day before, in increasing detail) to help them prepare. It may also be worth contacting the airline and explaining that a passenger has AS. Some airlines go out of their way to help, even as far as having 'trial runs' where they go though the whole process.

Security can be difficult because it's such an unusual process. Talking through all the possibilities, such as being asked to take your shoes or belt off, having hand luggage searched, and putting precious belongings through the scanner, helps to prepare the person with AS. This way they will be more likely to cooperate without any fuss. This must be done in advance. Equally, some airports have express security, where (for an extra fee) you can go though a separate security checkpoint. This may be better as it is quicker, and has fewer people.

Most people find the actual flight is the easiest part. The motion on a plane can be unusual, but many aspies actually enjoy this. They may also be fascinated by the view through the window, because the visual perspective from that height can be spectacular. The main issue tends to be sensory – the recirculated air, the change in air pressure, or the noise. Noise can be dealt with through earplugs, but recirculated air and change in air pressure are harder to deal with. A warning of what it might be like can help.

When you finally arrive at your holiday accommodation, if your child with AS is anxious about being somewhere new, it's helpful to make it seem a bit more like home. Something that registers almost subconsciously as you go through the door is any scent. I remember my brother Jack saying he wanted to go home because the house we were renting smelt funny. It didn't smell bad or weird, it just smelt different from home. People with AS are often particularly sensitive to this. If there is an air freshener or room scent you use at home, it's a good idea to bring one to use in the place where you stay. The smell will still be different, but it will be less of a change.

Another common problem is sleeping in a different bed. The excitement of being on holiday doesn't help, but often a child with AS really notices the different bed linen and pillows. If you bring his usual bed linen from home to use on the new bed, this will make it feel much more familiar. Or just bring his own pillow from home.

What about the food? Food is nearly always different on holiday, particularly if you are going to another country. In the weeks before you go on holiday, it may be worth serving the kind of food you know you will get on holiday, just to get the family used to it. If your child with AS has a huge problem with the new type of food because of taste hypersensitivity, it's best not to make too much of an issue out of it. If necessary let your child just have the food they like, such as fruit, bread and cheese. If you self-cater in this country you could get a delivery of food from the same supermarket you use at home, assuming there is one within a reasonable distance. That way you can be sure the food is the same as at home. On the other hand, part of a holiday is trying new food (and probably not having to cook!) and it's important to remember the holiday is for the whole family, including you.

One problem I sometimes have on holiday is other people! Often at a popular holiday destination, there are lots of noisy children, and the whole environment can seem crowded and hectic. It can help if your actual accommodation is relatively quiet and secluded. A self-catering holiday in a house away from the business of a resort, but within easy travelling distance, can often work well. This reduces the need to interact with lots of strangers and allows aspie children time to just be themselves. It's particularly helpful to have quiet accommodation if you spend all day on a crowded beach or beside a busy pool, because people with AS need downtime away from other people.

Sometimes the lack of structure on holiday can be difficult. Aspies often like to know exactly what is going to happen and when it will happen, so it can be useful to have a rough itinerary. It also helps to have some familiar activities from home such as the computer or video games. This might seem a bit excessive and probably would not impress educationalists, but aspies often find it hard to know what to do when taken out of their usual environment. If you tell most children to go and play in the garden, they will eventually come up with something to amuse themselves, such as an imaginary game, or kicking a ball around. But a child with AS may, literally, have no idea what to do. I'm not suggesting that your child should spend all their time on holiday glued to a screen, but it can be useful to have something to occasionally fill in the gaps between holiday activities such as going to the beach or visiting attractions. It is also something familiar, which may help destress if they become anxious.

Some aspie children love all the usual beach activities, but others will just not really know what to do on the beach and will need some guidance. They will need to be shown how to build a sandcastle rather than just being able to watch other children and copy them. Sometimes on beaches another child will wander over and want to join in, which can work well but it can also cause friction. Aspies tend to want to follow their own plan rather than sharing. When Jack was a child we had to watch him carefully because if a toddler came over and 'borrowed' a spade or trod on a sandcastle, he would get angry. He didn't understand that the toddler was too young to know any better.

There are also one or two dangers on beaches. A child with AS can easily get absorbed in what they're doing and may not keep track of where their family is. On a crowded beach it can be very difficult to find your family once you have lost sight of them. Always show your child how to find you, for example by pointing out some kind of marker nearby. For example, 'We're near the steps and about halfway down the beach.' Even then, it may be necessary for you to keep track of where your child is, rather than relying on them to keep track of you. Most young children find this a bit tricky, but an AS child may still find this tricky when they are a bit older. The same is true for paddling or swimming in the sea. There are dangers for any child but for aspies who get engrossed in what they are doing, the dangers are greater.

One last thing to remember when going away is that the holiday is designed to be fun for everyone, and it won't be unless everyone has a chance to relax and do things they enjoy. So, while it's important to bear aspie needs in mind, it's also important for the aspie to learn to compromise and adapt. If you present the holiday as a kind of adventure for all the family, where there will be a chance to try new things, this may help to create the right kind of attitude.

7

SCHOOL

The Survival Guide

I think I could write a whole book on the subject of education (and probably will one day), but I can only spend a chapter on it now. First, I want to reiterate something that I said earlier in this book: teachers are rarely, if ever, the problem.

Often I hear parents say that the teachers don't know about Asperger syndrome, that they are not doing enough, that they aren't making an effort. While every profession will have a few bad eggs, most teachers are overworked, underpaid, and yet extremely dedicated to the students they teach. At the time of writing, there is no obligation for teachers to learn about autistic spectrum disorders. This means that sometimes they won't be able to understand your child; they may inadvertently make things worse. *All because they simply don't know enough about it.* I hope that some teachers will be reading this now, in which case this will, with any luck, give them a basic understanding of the difficulties we face and how to help. However, the most important thing for both parents and teachers to take away from this chapter is the need to maintain an open dialogue. I know many parents get frustrated, and go in with all guns blazing (which can sometimes work). However, I have found that 99 times out of 100 the best long-term solution is to work together.

So what will this chapter cover? Well, we will have a look at education in primary school and secondary school. At the end, I will also briefly look at college (which is like secondary school, only easier) and university (which can be a challenge). I will cover bullying in Chapter 8. Sensory issues also play a huge part in this area. Keep in mind that schools are very noisy places, with a lot of people bumping into each other, a lot going on and a lot of weird smells (and tastes!). Often school is where sensory problems manifest.

Throughout this chapter, I will be assuming that a medium to high level of support is always needed, from primary school right though to university. It is often the case that people will need less support as they go through their academic careers, in which case not everything I suggest needs to be done. Equally, for very high levels of support, more may need to be done, but I hope that, either way, you will be able to see where to go. The most important thing to remember, is this:

All it takes is a little bit of the right support.

CHOOSING A SCHOOL

You may not know that your child has Asperger syndrome when you choose an infant or primary school, as quite often children are diagnosed at a later point. It's more likely that you will know that your child has AS when choosing a secondary school. Also your choice of school may be governed by the fact that you have an older child who is already attending school, and it's easier to keep them both at the same place. However, if you can choose, what factors should guide your decision?

SPECIALIST PROVISION

If your child is already seeing some kind of specialist, for example a speech therapist or paediatrician, they may recommend a special school or an AS unit attached to a mainstream school, or a language unit attached to a mainstream school. Generally you need a statement of special educational need to get a place, and it's all quite a lengthy process, so make sure you ask about what should happen in terms of education really early. The places in this kind of provision are usually oversubscribed so you need to maximise your child's chance of getting one. It can be very frustrating if all the paperwork is not ready.

Even if you think you know which specialist provision you want your child to go to, it's always best to go and look for yourself, and see several different places. This gives you a better idea of what's available, so you can make legitimate comparisons. This also gives you a clear idea of why you are choosing a particular place, which is useful because sometimes the local authority might want to send your child somewhere different, so you may need to be able to justify why you think your choice is better for your child.

It is useful to ask how much time children spend in the unit. This can vary from school to school. In some schools the children spend most of their time in the unit, in others they spend most of their time in the mainstream class. It can also vary depending on the individual child's capabilities, and on their development during their time at the school. Any of these options can work well, but it's important to have some idea of what to expect.

Sometimes a specialist placement is located some distance away from your home. Jordan went to the language unit of a mainstream infant school which was a half-hour drive away. It's usually possible to get free transport, often a taxi or minibus, so the distance isn't too much of an obstacle. Even small children seem to adapt to this fairly readily. However, if the minibus has to pick up several different children from various locations, it's possible the journey will be quite long. When Jordan travelled by minibus his journey took over an hour each way, which makes for a very long day. He usually had a sleep during the return journey, which helped pass the time.

MAINSTREAM PROVISION

A lot of children with Asperger syndrome are not judged to need a specialist placement. They go into mainstream school, perhaps with support. If your child has a statement of special educational need, there is a requirement that the support recommended in the statement is provided, so you are in a strong position. However, lots of children with AS don't get a statement because they are too able. This means you have to rely on the school being prepared to recognise and understand your child's needs. It helps if you have paperwork from professionals stating what those needs are.

It's not always possible to have this kind of proof of your child's difficulties, particularly if your child is more able and the difficulties are subtle. Also, not everyone wants to get a formal diagnosis for their child. Quite a few children have AS traits, but perhaps not enough to 'qualify' for the label. If your child has no particular difficulties with learning but perhaps has a problem with anxiety, or with socialising or behaviour, the responses of different schools can vary a lot. Some schools are very willing to accept that a child has AS and understand that they may need support in one or more of these areas. Other schools may give any child who has difficulties in these areas some support but do not necessarily recognise and understand Asperger syndrome. A few schools can be quite dismissive of the problems of children with AS or may not even acknowledge that a child has AS. This is particularly tricky because the school is unlikely to be open with the parents about this.

So, if you are choosing a mainstream school, what should you look for? This depends a bit on your child. Some children with AS prefer a fairly formal style of schooling, because the rules tend to be clear. However, some children are a bit intimidated because the teachers tend to be quite firm. Some children like a more relaxed, informal style of teaching because the teachers seem more approachable. However, this type of school often emphasises creativity and group work, which may not be areas of strength for a child with AS. The situation is further complicated because individual teachers within a school may have different styles.

It's really useful to ask other parents what they think of a particular school. If you know a few people who have a child who attends that school, they can often give you a valuable insight into what the school is really like. It's worth asking what they particularly like about the school, and if there is anything they don't like. Their priorities may be different from your own. For example, it may turn out that they really like a particular school because it's strong on sports, whereas your own child is not particularly interested in sport. It's helpful to find out the reasons behind their opinions as it enables you to assess how relevant their views are.

It's important to visit several schools, as this gives you a much better idea how the schools compare with each other. Some infant and junior schools have what I can only describe as a happy buzz, and this is a good sign that it's a happy environment. The children in classrooms may be chatting a bit but they are getting on with their work. In the corridors the children are not too subdued but nor are they getting a bit wild or fractious. The teachers give the impression of getting on well with each other, and working well together. It may be unfair to judge all schools on this, because if the school is in a difficult area, the teachers may need to be a bit more formal in order to impose order. However, this happy buzz does seem to be a feature of most good schools.

If you can, it's very helpful to talk to the special educational needs coordinator (SENCO). Try to be open and honest about your child's strengths and weaknesses, and about any concerns you may have regarding how they will cope in the school environment. If the SENCO really listens and seems to understand what you are getting at, that is a good sign. If they seem familiar with the problems and have come across them before, it's encouraging. If the SENCO has a particular interest in AS, you know that he or she will take your child's difficulties seriously.

One option which can work is to send your child to a school that has a unit, even though your child doesn't actually have a place in the unit. The idea is that there will be relevant expertise in the school so that your child's needs will be understood. This may work quite well, but it could depend on living close enough to be within the school's catchment area. If the school is located further away, your child might still be considered for a place if you explained the situation to the staff and perhaps wrote an explanatory letter with your application form. In any case it's a good idea to talk to the teachers and see whether they think it would be helpful for your child to attend their school. Transport would probably be an important consideration in your decision as the local authority would not provide this. One other factor to consider is what will happen when your child gets to secondary school age. If your child is attending a primary school some distance from your home, most of their school friends will go to a secondary school local to them. The choice will be either to try to get your child into that secondary school, so that they can stay with their friends, or send them to a more local school to you.

Private schools are another option (but an expensive one). The decision to go to a private school should not be made lightly; however, I know some people with AS who do well in a private schooling environment. Here, since parents are paying the school directly, they are sometimes more likely to adapt to the child. The classes are often smaller, allowing for a more individual approach. Equally, teachers tend to be more experienced, and so may have come across AS before. It is also an environment where being really good at a subject is valued and admired, rather than a cause for teasing and bullying which you sometimes get in mainstream education. However, this is a very academically driven environment, and not all aspies are academic. For those who are, this can be a good environment for them; however, if they are not, then this may well be a bad option. I know one person who was undiagnosed until she left for university as the private schooling environment was well suited to her, and she was able to blend in. However, this is by no means suitable for all.

The golden rule when choosing schools is to remember that every child is different. What I have done here is just briefly explore a few options to try and make you aware of the breadth of provision. You need to (honestly) decide what school is best for your child. This can be hard, as it can mean admitting that your son or daughter is not 'normal', and will need some extra support, but the benefits in the long run when you get it right are huge.

STARTING AT A NEW SCHOOL

Many parents are not aware that their children have AS when they start school, but if you do know, it's important to prepare your child as they will probably not have a clear idea of what school is like. It can be helpful to talk about school, and perhaps look at children's books about starting school (www.sevenstories.org.uk has a great selection of children's books, including some on this issue). I think it is really important that a child sees the school at least once with their parents before they start attending. Some schools have induction mornings when the children go in, spend time with their new teacher and meet their new classmates. However, this is just as scary for aspies as a normal school day. So, even before this, it can be really helpful for you and your child to meet the teacher and have a look round the school. When Jordan was due to start school, the teacher from the language unit came to visit him at home. This not only helped Jordan, but also gave the teacher a clearer idea of what Jordan was like in his own environment. The teacher might visit the child at nursery or playgroup if they know the child has some kind of special need.

It's important that, as much as possible, your child knows what to expect, because often AS children can get quite anxious or angry if they assume certain things are going to happen, and then they don't. For example, if your child attends playgroup only in the morning, they may expect school to be the same. If your child knows what to expect they won't get into the situation of getting ready to go home, only to discover they have to stay for the afternoon. Try to talk about both the similarities and differences between playgroup and school in the weeks before your child starts school, to help give them clearer expectations. For example, at playgroup the teacher may not insist that everyone stops what they are doing to come and listen to a story, whereas in school all the children have to come and listen to the teacher. Some AS children can get quite annoyed at being expected to stop what they are doing when they are in the middle of something. We have a one-track mind, and so when we start something, we like to finish it. If we have to stop part-way through, we often feel we will have to start again from scratch. If children realise beforehand that this is not the way things are done at school, that anxiety and frustration can be avoided.

Vocabulary can also be important. Make sure your child understands phrases such as 'break time', 'line up', 'arms folded', 'legs crossed', and so on. Words such as 'PE', 'PE kit' and 'assembly' may be unfamiliar. Most children are good at picking up the meaning from the context or just by copying everybody else, but children with AS may not automatically do this.

There are some other things you can do to prepare your child for school. Getting a uniform early and wearing it a few times can be very useful – especially for kids who are hypersensitive to touch. It may take them a while to get used to the feel of the uniform and so getting them used to it early can be really helpful.

GETTING THE BEST OUT OF INFANT AND JUNIOR SCHOOL

It's important to have a good working relationship with your child's teacher and with the school SENCO. It's helpful to meet with them beforehand if this is possible. Obviously, they need to know if your child has AS or AS traits, because this will help them understand your child. It may not be helpful to go into a detailed explanation at this point (unless you are asked for this) but if the teacher knows that, for example, your child can get very anxious if they don't understand something, or that they tend to understand instructions in a very literal way, this helps the teacher to make sense of your child's behaviour.

If the teacher is unfamiliar with Asperger syndrome and wants to find out more, there are various books which are useful. Tony Attwood's (1998) *Asperger's Syndrome: A Guide for Parents and Professionals* is one of the earliest practical books on Asperger syndrome and is still one of the best. Teachers are often trying to put Asperger syndrome into a nutshell. However, Aspergers is so complex and covers so many different areas of life that it makes it almost impossible to give a nice short definition of it.

FOLLOWING CLASS INSTRUCTIONS

Many children with AS cope very well with school and enjoy learning. However, there are some areas that may cause an aspie a few difficulties. Sometimes a child with AS can get into trouble for seeming not to listen properly when the teacher addresses the class as a whole. This can have various causes. It could be because the child is very anxious, particularly if they are in a new situation. Anxiety makes it hard to take in what is being said. Alternatively, some aspie children seem to take longer to realise that if the teacher is talking to the class, that includes themselves. If the teacher doesn't address them personally they don't understand that what is being said is relevant to them.

If an instruction is complex, they may need to be told individually what to do. For example, junior school children are sometimes given instructions which say that if you are in one group you need to do this, or, if you are in another group, you need to do that, and when you have completed the task you should work on another specific task. This can be quite difficult for a child with AS to make sense of. By the time they have heard the last instruction they have mentally lost the first. It can help if the teacher writes instructions down on the whiteboard, or if he or she tells the child individually what to do. Best of all is writing it down. Having stuff written down for us (either in words or pictorial form) can be so useful!

The opposite problem can also occur, when a child will take very personally something addressed to the class as a whole. For example, if the class is told off for chatting when they were meant to be working, a child with AS might get quite indignant because he was not chatting. One time Jordan's teacher asked the children not to waste the glue sticks because otherwise there would eventually be no glue sticks left to use. He came home and told Mum he needed to bring in a glue stick or enough money to buy a new one, when, in reality, the teacher had no expectation that he should do that.

Occasionally a child with AS can get into trouble because of their literal way of understanding language. For example, if the teacher says, 'Put your pencils down,' most children understand that to mean, 'Stop what you are doing and listen to me,' whereas a child with AS may ignore this because he is using a pen or a crayon rather than a pencil. Or a teacher may say, 'Fingers on lips,' meaning, 'Everybody stop talking and put your index finger up against your lips in a "Ssh" sign like me.' Most children understand this quite readily, but a child with AS might put all his fingers on his lips, or may put his finger on his lips but carry on talking. This is sometimes misinterpreted as trying to be clever or trying to be funny, or just ignoring instructions, when it may actually just be a very literal understanding of the teacher's words.

Academically children with AS are often capable of doing well, but there are areas of strength and difficulty. Also they are sometimes hampered by specific learning difficulties such as dyslexia. It often takes longer for children with AS to 'find their feet' educationally and be able to make the most of their intelligence, talent and ability to focus. This can be quite frustrating because other children seem able to do things easily which an AS child finds difficult, despite their best efforts. This is partly because the school environment imposes more strain on AS children than on other children. The social aspect of school may not be easy and straightforward for them, and there are often sensory issues which an AS child finds distracting and tiring.

Quite often children with AS have some difficulty with areas of the curriculum that need imagination. For example, Jordan doesn't really enjoy listening to stories. At infant school the stories are usually short and simple, with lots of pictures, and are therefore easy to follow. But in junior school the teacher might read stories which span several chapters and may not have any pictures. Jordan finds them difficult to follow, not only because he isn't able to imagine what's happening in the story, but also because these kind of stories require children to process lots of verbal material. This can be tricky for a child with AS: not only is it a fictional story (which requires understanding intentions, feelings and thoughts of others), but also it is being told in a very social manner. Jordan can read quite well, but he wouldn't read for pleasure because he isn't able to engage with the story by using his imagination. In general, children with AS often prefer factual books.

Often children have to do imaginative writing as part of a project. For example, if the subject of the project was the Second World War, they might be asked to write an account of being an evacuee, as if they themselves were the evacuees. This does require a certain amount of insight into what the thoughts and feelings of an evacuee might be, and this kind of social imagination is often difficult.

Comprehension exercises can also involve social imagination. These usually involve reading a simple story, or an extract from a story, and answering various questions about it. Most children with AS can answer factual questions about the story. These are usually 'who', 'what' and 'where' questions, such as, 'Who was taking the dog for a walk?' or 'What did they do in the park?' Questions like 'Why did the boy get angry with his friend?' or 'How did he know it wasn't true?' are much more complex and, again, require insight into the character's thoughts and feelings. Often children with AS do develop a certain amount of imagination and social insight, but it is not something that comes easily to them.

Many (but not all) children with AS prefer the more logic-based subjects in the curriculum, such as Maths and Science, or fact-based learning such as finding out about a country or a period in history. However, with maths there can be a problem with generalising learning and applying it in different ways. So children may know their two times table, but if they are given a question such as, 'Five boys each have two sweets, how many sweets are there all together?', they often don't realise they can use the two times table to work this out. Or they may not realise that dividing by two can also be done by using the two times table. Eventually maths can sometimes become an area of strength for an aspie, but applying it to a real life situation can still remain an area of weakness.

CREATING AN ASPIE-FRIENDLY SCHOOL ENVIRONMENT

The social and sensory aspects of school often prove quite challenging for a child with Asperger syndrome. However, there are some changes a school could make in order to create a more aspie-friendly environment. Often these changes help children who may not have AS, for example those who sometimes find the noise and bustle of school difficult, or those for whom English is a second language. Aspie-friendly measures are often generally good practice in schools.

It's helpful to have a quiet place where children can go at break times, such as the library. Most children relax at these times by chatting to friends in the playground, playing football or playing some other physical game such as tag. Children with AS often find these activities quite taxing. The way they relax is by going somewhere quiet where they don't have to socialise. Have you ever been at work and gone for a coffee, not because you wanted one, but because you needed to get up, stretch your legs and let your mind rest for a few minutes? We all need time to let our brain cool down, and run on autopilot for a while. The ideal would be to have a quiet room with a few activities such as Lego or board games, and it would be supervised by a helper who could join in, just be there to chat, or more often, do nothing and let the child do what they need to do.

In the classroom pupils usually have trays where they store their work and books. It's often a busy area, and it can be quite daunting to try to get a needed piece of work from your tray, especially as usually everyone needs to get their work at the same time. Keeping the tray in a quieter area, or having a tray on one side rather than in the middle of all the other trays can help. When we go to get our work, we have two conflicting drives. One is the need to do it quickly: if we are the last one people will look at us, and the teacher may get cross. The other drive is to not join in the scrum of children jostling to get their work. The whole thing is made easier if our tray is somewhere that is easily accessible.

It helps us if there are lots of visual prompts, because often AS children are less able to process and retain lots of verbal information. For example, when children are new to a building or classroom it helps if things are labelled. The cupboard where the art things are kept, the drawer where the measuring tools are kept, the place to put homework, can all have picture labels. Most schools do this anyway.

We like to know what is going to happen, so it's helpful if a brief itinerary is written down somewhere (on the whiteboard or on paper). This is particularly important where a routine has yet to be established. Work instructions can be written in the form of a brief list on the whiteboard. This is helpful because children with AS often find it more difficult to process and retain verbal information, especially when they are anxious. They may forget what the teacher told them to do, or just remember the first or last instruction. We like to know what is going to happen, so it makes us less anxious if a short itinerary is written up. This helps us to be able to anticipate the next event, so that it doesn't take us by surprise. Sometimes children with AS have a problem with a change of activity, particularly if they are engrossed in something, so being forewarned helps.

LUNCH TIMES

Lunch time is often very stressful. Lunch halls are usually busy and noisy. If there is a degree of choice about the food, you have to decide what you want quickly, and it can be tricky carrying a loaded plate and finding a place to sit. Quite a few aspies are fussy eaters, and often they will leave most of their food if it is food they don't particularly enjoy, especially if they are feeling quite stressed. But not eating much can cause them to feel tired and irritable in the afternoon.

A packed lunch can work well. You can put in food that you know your child will eat, and it is easier to check whether it is actually getting eaten. It is also more easy for your child to carry a packed lunch in a crowded dining hall. Sometimes in fine weather children are allowed to take their packed lunch outside on to the field or playground, away from the bustle of the lunch hall.

BEHAVIOUR

Most children with AS try to behave well because they are anxious about breaking the rules. Often it helps to have a short list of class rules written up and displayed somewhere so that they can be referred to. It's good if positive injunctions are included, such as 'Be kind and helpful'. Sometimes an aspie gets confused because other children are breaking a rule. For example, if the class has been told previously that there should be no running in the corridor, but on this occasion some of them are running, the aspie may think the rule no longer applies. If the rule is written up somewhere, this makes it more certain and permanent for an aspie. It can also help to explain rules (including any exceptions) to children. Sometimes we may simply not understand them, others we may need guidance as to when rules apply, what happens when they are broken, etc.

COMMUNICATION

It's important to have good communication with the school. Often when children with AS come home from school, they are not keen to talk about what happened that day. This can be because they are tired, or because nothing very remarkable happened. We generally don't see the point in talking about something just for the sake of chatting. Most importantly, we often like to keep home and school quite separate, so that when we come home we can switch off and forget about school.

The problem is that parents sometimes feel 'in the dark' about what is going on at school. This can be particularly true if the local authority provides your child with transport to school, because you don't chat to other parents at the school gate. If you want to ask the teacher something, you have to make a special journey or phone or email the school.

Some schools will provide a 'home school' journal for children with special needs, particularly if they have a specific communication problem and/or are quite young. Jordan had one when he was at the language unit at infant school, but it was less necessary at junior school. The teacher or classroom assistant can write down anything of note in the journal, and you can write down any questions or concerns you might have. It's also helpful to the teacher if you write down anything interesting your child has been doing, such as going on an outing or visiting grandparents. Often infants are asked to write a sentence or two about what they did over the weekend, and even if your child is not at that stage yet, it gives the staff ideas on what to talk about with your child, or what to ask them to draw.

It's not unusual for children with AS to neglect to give their parents letters from school and forms that need to be filled in, perhaps because once they are home they want to forget about school. It's always a good idea to check their bag. Otherwise you may only find out that your child needs to take some special item into school just before you are about to leave for school in the morning. Once my mother searched through Jack's bag for a vital form, only to discover some cakes crushed up at the bottom of his bag. He had made them at school probably a week or so before, and hadn't thought to mention they were in there!

It's important to have a good relationship with your child's teacher and SENCO. Like all of us, they respond well to respect and appreciation. At the same time you need to be honest about any serious concerns you may have. One way of doing this is to explain what you are worried about, the reasons why you are worried, and then to ask the teacher's opinion. For example, at one time my mother was worried that Jordan was being made miserable by a particular friendship at school. He would come home quite angry and say he hated a particular boy and hated school. When she talked to the teacher she discovered that Jordan and the other boy actually got on quite well together most of the time, but occasionally fell out with each other. So on this occasion the worries were unfounded. However, if you think your concern is being dismissed too lightly, you may need to monitor the situation with your child. If you find that your original concern remains, go back and explain why you are still worried. If it turns out that there is a problem and you have an idea of what might help, it may be best to say something like, 'I was wondering if [insert your suggestion] might help. I don't know, what you think?' Teachers at the infant and junior level usually get to know the children in their class very well and are keen to sort problems out if they can.

SENSORY ISSUES

Noise and the busy environment seem to be the main sensory issues for children with AS. The playground is often very busy, with children running in different directions and calling to each other.

This can be a bit disorientating for children with AS until they get used to it. Sudden loud noises such as the school bell or the teacher's whistle seem to startle aspies more than other children. A short, sharp noise that is unexpected startles the hypersensitive among us much more than it would other children. Anything that involves very loud noise can be difficult. One lesson that Jordan had involved a drumming demonstration, and the teacher had to take him out because he was getting distressed. Collective shouting can also be difficult; sometimes teachers ask the whole class to shout back a response, and often it's the child with AS who will have his fingers in his ears. To a certain extent these things can't be avoided, and usually an aspie learns to cope over time. Loud noises are much less of a problem for Jordan now that he is a bit older. However, it helps if the teacher is aware of the difficulty and doesn't tell the child not to be silly.

CHILDREN WHO HAVE DIFFICULTIES IN MAINSTREAM EDUCATION

There are children who have particular difficulties in fitting in to a normal school environment, but who are generally not considered for units or special schools because they academically able. Some children with Asperger syndrome are extremely bright. The problem is that sometimes these children become intensely frustrated and this is often apparent in angry outbursts in class. The issue does not seem to be only that they may need more challenge in the work they are doing. It almost seems as if they are so focused and intense about everything they do, that they become very intolerant when anything is not 'right'. They can even get angry and upset with other children in the class if they are not doing their work the correct way.

For some children like this the AS traits seem to become intensified. For example, they may react very strongly to noise or to unexpected deviations from the routine. If the teacher makes a mistake or does something to which the child takes exception, the child may start arguing heatedly with the teacher, and may be egocentric in understanding the situation. The problem can sometimes be with providing work which interests and challenges the child while managing other behavioural issues.

Initially it can seem that the child is just being a bit unreasonable. If the child gets angry with other children over some minor issue, for example, it may seem as if the child just needs a little guidance about not getting into big quarrels over things that don't really matter. However, over time it becomes apparent that they really cannot stop themselves and cannot just calm down and let an issue drop. Sometimes, if concessions are made in order to help the child cope, such as allowing them to sit at a table on their own, they may then start to insist that further measures are taken, such as not allowing anyone to sit near this table.

This can be very frustrating for the parents and the teacher. This child's behaviour seems self-defeating as everyone can see that the child has great potential. However, they are genuinely unable to fit in with an ordinary class. People tend to assume that because the child is highly intelligent they must be quite mature and be able to reflect on their own behaviour and control it. But often there is a big disparity between the child's general intelligence and their social and emotional intelligence.

There are children with AS who seem very bright and may have an advanced vocabulary for their age. They may almost come across as 'little professors', and have impressive conversations with adults about their favourite subjects. However, they really struggle with even the basics of reading, writing and maths. It's easy to jump to the conclusion that they are not really trying, particularly as they often get distracted by quarrels with other children. It may be that this kind of child is held back by a specific learning disability such as dyslexia or dyspraxia. Dyspraxia can result in a child having very poor pencil control, which affects handwriting. This may not be recognised as quickly as it might be in another child, because the child is so intelligent.

Sometimes a child like this can start to avoid doing the work, probably because they feel embarrassed and humiliated by their difficulties. It can be very hard to labour at producing a small amount of written work in 'babyish' handwriting, possibly with lots of spelling errors, when other children who seemingly aren't as bright easily produce a whole page of perfect work. So a child with these difficulties will sometimes wander around the classroom 'looking for a pencil', or may pick a quarrel with another child, just to delay the awful moment when they have to sit down and start grappling with the work. These children are often quite isolated socially because of their 'little professor' manner, and other children may deliberately annoy them because they are so easily wound up.

Sometimes, they may deliberately not try, as they do not see why they need to. If it isn't Thomas the Tank Engine, or Pokémon, then they don't see the point in it. Motivating a child with AS who does not see the point in work, and does not understand the long-term benefits, can be challenging.

There are also children with AS who are academically able who are unable to cope with a normal school environment. They may become extremely upset and anxious in school, and this anxiety doesn't seem to reduce over time. In fact it may increase because other children start noticing that these children are behaving differently and start to avoid them or tease them. Issues that started out as minor problems become things that these children dread so that they are having lots of major upsets in school. Alternatively, the AS child may seem to cope while in school but become very upset about school when at home.

It's often difficult to know how to respond to a child's continuing misery, though clearly it's important to remain encouraging and supportive. Lots of children do go through times when they hate school. Some children can be quite extreme in what they say, for example, 'I hate school and I wish I was dead!' Occasionally children may be keeping up the emotional pressure in the hope that in the end they won't have to go to school. However, sometimes a child can become completely crushed and overwhelmed by the whole school experience.

In all these cases maintaining a good working relationship between school and home is vital. It's very important that both have a clear understanding of the child's difficulties. For example, if it's assumed that the child is just being lazy, or difficult, or naughty, with no recognition of Asperger syndrome, the reasons behind the child's behaviour will be misunderstood. If this happens it's important to get an independent professional assessment of the child, which I hope will clarify this issue. Once the problems are understood, it is more likely that the school will be able to try strategies that may be effective.

It's important to try to avoid the situation where the parents are blaming the school and the school is blaming the parents, and both become defensive. It's much better to try to have an attitude of, 'Let's work together to see what we can achieve.' This can be difficult to maintain when lots of strategies have been tried and both parents and teachers are becoming frustrated and demoralised. But when parents and teachers stop really listening to each other, nothing can be achieved.

It's worth trying a variety of strategies, giving each one a fair time to work before dismissing it. Sometimes one change might make a big difference. For example, sometimes just having a quiet room available during break times can help. Some schools have what I call 'Get out of jail free' cards. Here the child is given a card which they can show their teacher when they are finding the classroom situation too difficult. The idea is that the child can go to a quiet room for ten minutes in order to calm down. This can work well but does require a certain maturity from the child. Otherwise they might be tempted to use it just to get out of the lesson.

Any particular strategy may not solve all the problems but might make enough difference to enable children to cope, or to enable them to be more cooperative in the classroom. It's also worth getting advice and consulting people who have experience in the field and may have good suggestions. If you can find other parents who have a child with similar difficulties, they can tell you what worked or did not work for them, and also be a source of support for you.

The child's academic ability can actually work against them when trying to get extra help funded by the local authority. For example, it can be very difficult to get a statement of special educational need, which would probably entitle your child to extra help, if your child is educationally able, even if the school recognises that it is unable to meet the child's needs within its own resources. It may be helpful to consult your local parent partnership service. Every local authority in the UK has one, and it can be found at www.parentpartnership.org.uk.

However, for a few children, despite everyone's best efforts, mainstream school eventually becomes unworkable. Either the child really cannot cope with school, or the school can no longer cater for the child. It's possible that the child could be considered for a place in a unit within a mainstream school, because of the proven difficulties they have within an ordinary class. Another option is to look for a specialist school. There are various types of school for children with AS, although there are far fewer than are needed. It can be difficult to find a match between a specialist school and your child's academic ability, particularly if your child is extremely clever. It can also be a battle to persuade the local authority to agree to fund a place.

A final option is to take your child out of school completely. Obviously this is not a choice to take lightly, as every child has to be educated, so you would need to either educate your child at home or find some other means of educating them. In some circumstances the local authority has to provide a certain amount of tuition at home. For example, when I had a prolonged breakdown because I could no longer cope with school, the psychiatrist agreed that I was too ill to attend school. The local authority was then obliged to provide five hours of tuition per week. There are also some internet-based learning courses, which may be appropriate, depending on the age of your child. It's important to find out as much as you can about what help and support is available before taking your child out of school. It is possible to educate your child yourself, although this does become much more difficult at secondary school age. There may even be a local home schooling group which meets up occasionally for activities. However, it is a big commitment, and it can be very draining to be with your child all day, every day, particularly if you are trying to get them to do work that they don't really want to do.

CHOOSING A SECONDARY SCHOOL

Applications for secondary school usually have to be completed in the first six weeks or so that your child is in Year 6, so you really need to start thinking about secondary schools quite early. (Year 6 is for children aged between 10 and 11.) You can learn a lot by talking to people whose children attend various secondary schools. Often different people have a different experience of the same school, and this reflects the fact that some children will thrive in a particular school but some will have problems. This may be due to difficulties with friendship groups and/or difficulties with the work. The problems with friendship groups tend to be either a lack of a friendship group, which leaves the child isolated and vulnerable to bullying, or the wrong friendship group, which influences the child to misbehave, and often leads to problems with school work. It's true that these problems can occur in any school, because it depends on the other children in your child's class. However, it can be revealing to see how the schools deal with any problems, and other parents may have some first-hand knowledge of this. Some schools will tend to have a 'sink or swim' attitude. They concentrate on the able majority and see any difficulties, particularly social difficulties, as the child's own problem. Other schools do have a more caring ethos and are more willing to listen and work with parents if problems occur.

If there is a local autism or Asperger syndrome parent support group in your area, then these groups can often be a good source of information and advice. You may be able to find other parents who have direct experience of sending a child with AS to a particular secondary school. It's interesting to find out the level of support that was given and the school's general attitude. However, different people can have different experiences of the same school, so keep an open mind.

In the autumn term many schools invite parents to see around the school during a typical day, and often they are shown around by one or two pupils. This is a good opportunity to see what the school is like, and to ask lots of questions. It's interesting to talk to the children showing you around, and get a first-hand perspective of what the school is like. If you ask questions such as, 'What's the best thing and the worst thing about the school?' and 'Do you get to do any good activities at the end of term?' you often gain an insight into what school life is like. However, be warned that staff may intervene on difficult questions, or that children may have been briefed. It's usually possible to take your child with you on these tours. This can work well, but it may be a bit intimidating. Some secondary schools are very large (mine had 10 classes of 30 in each year), and when the bell rings to change lessons the corridors are flooded with hoards of big, noisy teenagers.

Often all the parents who are considering sending their child to a particular school attend a talk by the head teacher about the school. Most secondary schools seem very impressive from this perspective. Parents are left with the idea that it would be a privilege for their child to be accepted there. There is apparently no bullying and the pupils have wonderful educational opportunities. I'm sure no one is trying to deceive parents but it's important to bear in mind that the head teachers want to present their schools in the best light. It probably is a very successful school, but there is often a bit of a gap between what the school aspires to achieve and the day-to-day reality. Remember that for schools, the more children they take, the more money they get, hence sometimes getting the hard sell.

As with choosing a primary school, it's really important to talk to the SENCO. Tell them about your child and explain any particular areas of concern. It's interesting to learn if the SENCO has experience of a child with similar difficulties or whether they have a particular interest in this area. Even if they don't, a willingness to listen and take your concerns seriously is a good sign.

When finally deciding on a particular secondary school, there are lots of factors to be taken into account. You may want your child to go to the same school as their friends from primary school. Having friends from primary school who are starting at the same secondary school can make a big difference, as the child feels much less isolated. However, quite often schools tend to distribute children from the same school in several different classes, so there may only be one or two who are in the same lessons, and often friendship groups change in the new environment. Even so, having familiar faces to hang around with at break time can be very reassuring. You may want your child to attend the same school as an older brother or sister. It can help your child to have some 'insider knowledge' about the school, and often gives your child a more realistic idea of what to expect. On the other hand, you may need to be careful that the older sibling doesn't take advantage of the situation by alarming your younger child with stories of just how terrible school is!

If the school has a good academic reputation this is obviously encouraging, but I would also look for a school that has a strong sense of being a community, and a caring reputation. This probably means that the school isn't huge, and that it values each individual not only on the basis of their academic ability. Some outwardly successful schools are really only interested in the children who are confident, outgoing and able. A school that has discipline problems is not likely to be able to protect a vulnerable child from bullying and exploitation.

PREPARING FOR TRANSITION TO SECONDARY SCHOOL

Once you have decided on a school and gone through the application process, it's important to make contact with the SENCO again. He or she may have a general understanding of Asperger syndrome, but will not know your child. What I think can be really useful is to compile a small document giving relevant information about your child. This could explain what your child finds difficult, approaches that have helped solve these problems, and also your child's strengths. You could ask his or her teacher for feedback about what they have found helps or makes things worse with your child, and anyone else whose opinion might be valuable, such as the SENCO at the current school. You could also include a copy of any reports, for example from a psychologist, that you think would be helpful in understanding your child. This would give the SENCO at the new school a much clearer picture of what your child is like.

It's important to find out what measures can be put in place within the secondary school to help your child. Children who have a statement of special educational need may be entitled to a certain level of support, depending on the statement's recommendations, though often statements avoid being specific about this. Many schools like to just wait and see how a child copes in the school environment. This way, as they see it, the school provides support only if it is really needed. However, it's worth making the point that if a child is allowed to struggle for too long when they are really not coping, it can be quite difficult to rescue the situation. The child loses all confidence and can become completely overwhelmed. It's important that you know what the SENCO recommends you do if you start to notice problems, so the situation doesn't escalate.

If your child hasn't seen round the school, it may be possible to arrange to be shown around. It's best if this is at a relatively quiet time during the school day, or even after school. If your child can meet the SENCO this is also helpful as it will be a familiar face when he or she starts school and someone your child can turn to if things get difficult. Most schools have an induction day or half-day during the summer term, where children meet their new form teacher, see their form room, and get a clearer idea of what to expect when they start. This is helpful, although a child with AS often finds it difficult to take in all this new information. A map of the school and a timetable (even if it's just an example timetable from the previous year) are very useful. In the weeks before school starts, you can take a look at them with your child and help them to become familiar with the timings of the day, and the routes from their classroom to the various buildings. This should enable your child to feel a bit more prepared for the first day of school.

STARTING SECONDARY SCHOOL

Nearly all children find that secondary school is very different from primary school, and most find the first few weeks a fairly exhausting time. At primary school a child normally has, perhaps, two or three different teachers in each year, and those teachers get to know each child very well. In secondary school there is usually at least one different teacher for each subject, and that teacher probably teaches hundreds of different children. There are lots of different classrooms, probably in several different buildings. Each child is expected to get to the right place with the right books at the right time. Then, when they come home tired from a long day, there are usually a couple of pieces of homework to do. This is a lot to assimilate, and often the teachers are quite strict because they want to set high expectations for behaviour.

Socially, the child goes from being one of the big kids at primary school, to being just one of hundreds of pupils, most of whom are big, loud, and a bit intimidating. The social environment becomes more harsh, because it is less within the control of the teachers. In primary school the teachers are usually aware of the changing alliances, the children who are being left out and the children who are being bullied. To a certain extent they can try to manage the situation to make things easier for the children who are having a hard time. In secondary school the teachers are much less aware of what is going on. As a result there can be much more cattiness among the girls and a lot of boys start to act big and tough.

Overall, each child has a much greater responsibility for himself or herself. They have to become much more organised, remembering what they need to put in their bags for the day ahead. They have to make note of important information given in the lessons, such as the homework tasks. They have to stay reasonably alert throughout the day, remembering where they need to go for each lesson, switching quickly from one subject to the next. They also have to manage lunch times, choose what to buy from the canteen and making sure they have enough money to pay for it. Finally they have to get the homework done or face the consequences. This means there is not much opportunity to just relax and unwind. I remember back when I started at secondary school I often felt as if I had been drafted into the army.

The challenges posed by secondary school are sometimes particularly difficult for people with Asperger syndrome. We often find it difficult to organise ourselves, so we sometimes forget to pack the right books for the right day. We can find it difficult to switch our attention flexibly, so we may not realise the teacher is telling the class what to do for homework if we are busy working on the task set for the lesson. When we move on to the next lesson, we may still be preoccupied with some problem that occurred in the previous lesson. There are more people to mix with and social situations are always difficult for us to 'read', especially when we are already under pressure with school work.

It does get easier after a few weeks. You get into a routine, you become familiar with the location of the different buildings and classrooms, and, I hope, you also find a few friends.

One way in which parents can make things a bit easier is by helping their child to get organised. Most children need help with this to start with, but children with AS often need more help for longer because they get more stressed by the whole new-school situation. At home put a spare copy of the school timetable in a place that can easily be seen; my sister has her timetable stuck on the fridge with fridge magnets. Then it's easy to see what is needed for the next day. Try to get your child to pack their bag in the evening rather than waiting until the morning. That way if there are any problems, such as missing PE kit, there is more time to sort them out. Check that your child also has money, if they need it for school lunch. This may seem a bit overprotective, but it helps to avoid unnecessary hassles and upsets.

HOMEWORK

It's quite important to get into a routine with homework. If there is a time when it is usually done and a place where it is usually done, it becomes more of a habit. I always tried to do homework in break times at school or as soon as I got home. That way I knew I could forget about school until the next day. However, this probably isn't the best system, because spending break times doing homework can make you quite isolated socially, and it means that during the day you just don't get a break.

Many schools have a homework club at the end of the school day. It's a large room where students can go to do their work, usually with access to computers, because quite a lot of homework involves finding things out on the internet or typing work on a computer and then printing it out. This can be a good option as often we need to keep home life and school life very separate, though the prospect of extending the school day in this way is probably not appealing.

Some students like to do their homework as soon as they get home, to get it out of the way. That is what I did, if I couldn't get it all completed during school breaks. However, most people really need a bit of rest and relaxation before they start work on it. Perhaps the important thing is just to have a time when it's usually done, for example before the evening meal, so that you get into a routine. This helps to avoid the situation where you have to keep nagging your child to do it, and they keep putting it off. Some kids like to extend their school schedule to home, and have a homework schedule, which can work really well. Try to make sure the environment is really boring and there are no distractions. It's also useful if you are available to help if necessary, as there often seem to be minor problems that need sorting out.

Some people advocate having a special place set up in the child's bedroom where they can go and do homework. This may work for some students, particularly those who are doing serious studying for GCSEs. But most 11-year-olds are not keen on this arrangement, and in any case probably need access to a computer and a helpful adult. However, in some circumstances this may be the best option.

Sometimes a piece of homework does not have to be handed in to the teacher until the next lesson in that subject, which could be a week away. It's usually best to do it on the day that it's set. That way the lesson material is still fresh in your child's mind, and your child doesn't run the risk of forgetting to do it. If there are problems with the homework, this gives you time to sort them out; often teachers can be contacted by email if you have a query about the homework. There are times when it's better to leave the homework for another day, for example, if your child has too much homework on one day, but encourage your child to make a note of this (and make a note of it yourself) to make sure it isn't overlooked.

My personal opinion (that I know is shared by several autism professionals) is that since an AS child is having to work twice as hard to meet with the social, the communicative, the sensory *and* the academic demands of school, they should be exempted from homework, on the grounds that they need to rest! Understandably, many teachers are against this, and for good reason. During A levels, a large proportion of learning is home study based. Certainly at degree level, 80–90 per cent of my time spent working is independent, not taught. Homework helps build up this independent work skill, and clearly has a role to play. Often, I advocate a compromise. Either dropping a non-core subject (languages, for example), and using that time for homework, or reducing the amount or difficulty of homework tasks. However, changing the curriculum is not a decision to be taken lightly, and must be agreed by the parents (the experts on their children) and the teachers (the experts on education).

ASPERGER AWARENESS

If you have been in contact with the school's SENCO, he or she should have made all the members of staff who teach your child aware of your child's particular difficulties. However, the extent to which these members of staff will understand the difficulties and be willing to take them into consideration can vary. Partly this is because, in a large school, each teacher has so many different classes with so many different pupils, so they may just forget that a particular child in one of these classes has certain difficulties. Also they may need to tailor their teaching style to suit the majority of children, so, for example, they may need to be a bit intimidating in order to keep control of the class, even though it may make the person with AS quite stressed. Having taken that into account, there are a few teachers who are unwilling to make any allowances for children who are not quick to understand and follow instructions.

As in primary schools, good teaching practice for children with AS is usually good teaching practice for most children. It's important that teachers are very clear when giving instructions such as what homework needs to be done and when it needs to be done by. It's even better if they write the instructions up on the whiteboard, so they can be seen as well as heard. Pupils need time to write homework instructions down; sometimes they are given in the last minute of the lesson, which is a problem for children who don't write quickly because they end up late for the next lesson.

Some children with AS can have a problem with taking notes during the lessons. It can be difficult for them to pick out the important details, particularly if the teacher tends to tell them a lot of information. They sometimes try to write everything down, and then they are unable to keep up with what the teacher is saying, or they try to write really fast and then their handwriting becomes illegible, even to themselves. It is actually quite a difficult skill to listen and write at the same time, particularly if you have to sift the information in order to pick out the important points. It involves doing two things at once, whereas aspies cope much better when they focus on one thing. A further problem can occur when pupils have to revise from their notes for a test. If the notes are illegible or miss out important points, it's impossible to revise effectively. Here it helps if the pupil is allowed to take the textbook home for revision. Some schools seem to have a general policy of taking in textbooks at the end of each lesson, probably because this avoids the problem of pupils losing textbooks and the school having to pay for replacements. However, if a child has genuine difficulties with writing notes, it should be possible for an exception to be made.

SPECIAL MEASURES FOR PEOPLE WITH ASPERGER SYNDROME

The amount of help children with AS get varies, depending partly on their degree of impairment, partly on the resources of the school, and perhaps partly on how Asperger-aware the school is. If your child has a statement of special educational need, this should stipulate what help they should get. It also means that the local authority will provide the school with a certain amount of funding for this help. In some cases pupils with AS might be given one-to-one support for most of the day. This tends to happen when it's recognised that it would be very unlikely that the children would be able to manage the day on their own. For example, if they would be unable to follow the lesson and write down the homework without someone there to prompt them, or if they probably would not be able to navigate themselves around the school in order to get to each lesson, they would need this kind of support. This also may be granted if they had behavioural problems related to AS, for example if they were often very angry and confrontational whenever they became stressed or confused.

Many children with Asperger syndrome don't have a statement of special educational need, in which case the amount of help a child will get is less certain. What often seems to happen is that a classroom assistant will be put with a class where there are a few children who may need a bit of extra help, and he or she will give help when necessary. As children get older they often don't like to be seen by their peers as having 'special needs' and being in need of special assistance, so a bit of discreet help shared between a few children can work quite well. However, a lot depends on whether the classroom assistant understands the problems which a particular child has.

It can also help to have a person that pupils with AS can go to if they are worried and need help, and/or a room to which they can retreat. Often just knowing that there is a person you can go to if necessary is reassuring. The only problem with this is that it may be difficult for the aspie to find this person, unless there is a specific time and place where he or she can normally be found.

When I was having problems at secondary school I was given what I call a 'Get out of jail free' card. This was a card I could show to the teacher if I was becoming overwhelmingly anxious. It explained that I could leave the lesson because I was finding things too difficult. The disadvantage of this is that you have to actually get out of your seat in the lesson and go up to the teacher to show him or her the card. If you are already in an anxious state and feeling overwhelmed, it can just be too difficult to do this. Also, the other people in the class notice what has happened and may later ask you just why you should be allowed this special concession. It is much better if the child is situated near the door, and can leave their card on their desk to explain their absence, making their exit much less conspicuous.

Some schools prefer not to provide any help for children with AS when they join the school. The thinking behind this is that they may be able to manage without any help, and, if they don't, help can be added at a later point. The problem with this is that if a child isn't able to cope, this can really damage their confidence and their whole attitude to school. I went to a school where they had this kind of approach and my experience was that, by the time some help was provided, it was really too late. I had become extremely anxious and depressed. I had no friends because I was permanently in an anxious and preoccupied state, and I hated school. The problem can be further complicated because an aspie may seem to be coping quite well at school, but is actually saving up all their anxiety and anger until they get home, which feels like the only safe place to express it. It can then be difficult for the parents to convince the school that their child needs more help, because the child always seems to be coping when at school. Even if parents explain how difficult their child is at home, the school may think that the behaviour at home is not caused by difficulties at school.

Perhaps the best solution, if a school advocates the 'wait and see how he copes' approach, is to ask what would be taken as evidence that the child is not coping. Sometimes the school does not have a clear idea about this, which makes it quite difficult to monitor how the child is faring. It's reasonable to expect the school to define its criteria for not coping, as this enables both you and the school to effectively monitor the situation. It may help to explain at the outset that it's possible for a child with AS to put up a good front at school and only show how difficult they are finding school when they get home. That way, if difficult and distressed behaviour emerges at home they may find it easier to accept it could be due to problems coping at school.

It's important to aim to have a good relationship with the school. If you are becoming concerned about something, it can help to email the SENCO or the relevant teacher. It is often difficult to reach a teacher by phone, and email gives you the opportunity to explain things clearly, and ask the teacher what he or she thinks. It also gives the teacher the chance to make a considered response. If the teacher suggests waiting to see if the problem sorts itself out, you can monitor the situation. Make a note of the times when the problem reoccurs, so that if you do need to go back to the teacher, you can give an objective picture of what's been happening. Another advantage of email is that you can keep a record of all the emails sent and received. It's often difficult to remember all the details of a phone conversation, whereas with email you can look at the text and check. The danger with emails is that it's possible to write and send one in haste when you're feeling quite angry and upset about an issue. It's nearly always best to wait until you've calmed down, so that you can put your case in a more considered way.

NEW SOCIAL SITUATIONS

An important part of the transition from primary to secondary school is adjusting to a very different social situation. Whereas it was relatively easy to find your friends in a primary school playground, in secondary school there are often various areas where kids can 'hang out' and a sea of people to negotiate. Even in lessons there may be different classmates for some subjects. The more people there are, the more you have to work out how you fit in.

The pupil–teacher relationship is different. At primary school the teacher is a bit like an aunt or uncle. He or she knows you well and makes allowances for the fact that you might sometimes forget to bring in the homework on the correct day, or not always have the right kit for PE. In secondary school the teachers are much more distant, partly because each teacher sees a particular class only once or twice a week, and then for only about an hour. They don't tend to make allowances for things like forgetting to hand in homework or for losing a part of your PE kit. This is because they know that if they don't set high expectations for everyone right from the start of the first term, it will be difficult to generally achieve reasonable standards of behaviour and cooperation later on. This means that if a pupil forgets things, he or she will probably get a warning, or a detention. This can be difficult for aspies, who are often a bit disorganised, and can easily be distracted by sensory issues and anxiety.

Teachers vary in their style. Some are more friendly, some are more intimidating, and some are fairly neutral. The pupils in a class are often fairly good at tuning in to the individual teacher, and knowing what they can get away with. So in some lessons they might chat more and fool around because they know they can get away with it. An aspie is more likely to be confused by the varying styles of different teachers. The result might be that an aspie doesn't talk in any lessons, even when a bit of chatting is allowed. This can look odd to other pupils. Or the aspie might choose the wrong lesson in which to be relaxed and chatty and get into trouble. There are so many different teachers, and so many different situations, it can be difficult to know how to behave.

The social situation is much more complex at secondary school. Lots of boys like to seem 'cool' by showing a relaxed disregard for authority and by not appearing to take learning too seriously. Girls often form tight friendship groups and make bitchy remarks. Generally the girls are disdainful of boys in their year, and the boys laugh at the girls. However, now that adolescence is kicking in, there are lots of rumours and teasing about who fancies who.

As parents will know, teenagers in general are very good at sarcasm, put downs, and making smart verbal retorts. This is seen a lot in secondary schools among peers, and makes it harder for a person with AS to know what is really being communicated. For example, it may be difficult for a person with AS to realise that when some girls at school come over to him and say, 'Wow, that's such a cool haircut!', they are actually making a joke about how rubbish his hair looks. A lot of banter goes on in classrooms, some of it fairly good natured, some of it quite cutting. Often if things get a bit boring the class loudmouth will try to make someone look a bit silly by making derogatory remarks about them that the whole class can hear. It sometimes helps to be able to make a smart remark back. This gains respect from the other people in the class, who see that you are able to give as good as you get and stick up for yourself. However, this kind of quick-witted verbal facility isn't easy for people with AS.

The use of swearing adds yet another complication to verbal interaction at school. Most children know a few rude expletives before they get to secondary school, but normally these aren't used very often. At primary school, if a teacher overhears a child swearing, that child is usually in big trouble. However, at secondary school lots of kids use expletives quite casually, partly because they think it gives the impression that they are cool and grown up. The problem for someone with AS is knowing when the use of bad language is appropriate and when it isn't. One option is to completely avoid using any expletives, but, sadly, this can mark you out as different from everyone else. However, if you use bad language in the wrong context, for example in front of a teacher, it will probably get you into trouble. This problem can also affect life at home, because the rules for when and when not to use a swear word are so complicated. Some families are fairly tolerant of bad language, other families will allow a bit of swearing when someone is angry or upset. However, this too can vary depending on whether young children or guests are present. The final complication is that some swear words are regarded as more offensive than others, and so much depends on which swear word you use.

THE CURRICULUM

Some subjects in the curriculum are well suited to people with Asperger syndrome. Subjects which are about understanding logical processes and remembering data, such as the sciences, can sometimes be areas of strength, and many aspies are good at IT. However, there are also aspies who find these subjects quite difficult. Generally, the good thing about secondary school is that eventually you get to concentrate on your strong subjects, but there can be a lot of plodding through subjects that don't really interest you before you get to that point.

There is often streaming in certain subjects. Streaming entails pupils being tested and assessed, and then put in a class with other children of similar ability for lessons in that subject. The advantage of this is that the lessons are more suited to the pupils' particular abilities. The disadvantage is that in the least able class, there are often some people who have lost all interest in school and who spend much of their time fooling about. This can make it difficult for the people who do want to learn. Sometimes aspies are put in this kind of class, because it seems right for their level of ability. However, quite often aspies under-perform at school because they get very anxious and are distracted by the noise and business of the general environment. They then get put in the class for less able children where there is often more noise and more distractions.

At school I was put in the least able stream for several subjects. It was only when I started doing A levels at college that I really began showing any academic strengths, probably because in this environment I had lots of support and the other people in the class mostly wanted to be there and wanted to learn. I'm not sure how this problem can be avoided, but it does seem harsh that some aspies end up in the most behaviourally difficult classes at school, perhaps partly because they are too stressed out to learn. Being in this kind of class is probably going to make them even more stressed. The only consolation is that the aspie may have hidden strengths and talents which could be brought out by the right environment.

A few people with AS eventually get to the point where they are really struggling to cope with school and are becoming ill. Like myself at that age, they have done their best, over an extended period of time, to adapt to secondary school life and to find ways of coping. However, eventually it becomes clear to everyone that they are buckling under the strain and their mental health is being seriously affected. In these circumstances it may be possible that the school will allow the person with AS to drop one or two of the less important subjects that they find particularly difficult. For example, I found PE very difficult. Because I am dyspraxic I have the coordination of a penguin on roller-skates. At that time I was also rather overweight because I was self-medicating for depression with chocolate. The result was that, for me, PE was a rather humiliating experience, which, in my already fragile state of mind, became excruciating. Fortunately my care was being overseen by people from Education Other Than At Schools (a department in the local authority) and they recommended to the school that I be allowed to drop PE in order to alleviate some of the stress. This helped me a lot.

COURSEWORK FOR GCSES

As students get older they are often given longer work projects to do, either at home, at school, or both. This is sometimes known as coursework, and has become more important because GCSEs currently involve quite a lot of coursework. It also gets the student used to working more independently. Usually this involves things like studying a particular topic, researching from a variety of sources, and presenting the information in various different ways.

I have a love/hate relationship with coursework. The good thing about coursework is that if you spend time and effort on it you can usually get a good mark, which is particularly important if it goes towards your final grade in a subject. Many aspies work best when they are given the opportunity to focus on one thing and explore it in depth. The less-good thing is that it usually requires quite a bit of self-organisation and self-motivation. Often we panic a bit and try to get the whole thing completed on the night it is set. Alternatively we leave the whole thing until the last minute and then have to work under a lot of pressure in order to get it done in time.

The best method seems to be to try to get a clear idea of what steps you need to take in order to complete the project. So, for example, if you have to write an essay on a particular subject, the first stage is probably to find out information, and the second stage might be work out roughly what you need to write in the essay. The third stage would be to work out the order in which you need to write things in the essay (such as the introduction, the facts, a discussion of the facts, and a conclusion) and the last stage would be to write the essay. The teacher will often have given

174

some idea of how to tackle the project, which helps you to work out what these steps are. Once you have broken the task down in this way, it is easier to see how much time each step will take. You can work on it one step at a time, and schedule in regular times to work on it.

EXAMS

Exams are a regular part of secondary school life, and as you progress through the school they become more important because they lead to recognised qualifications. Often schools encourage students to take up to ten GCSEs, which means that they will be taking exams in most of the subjects they have been studying from the time they entered secondary school. Many people with AS will have strong subjects and weak subjects, and there is probably more of a disparity in their abilities in different areas than there is for most students. Subjects which require insight and empathy, such as English Literature and Religious Studies, can be quite difficult for aspies. Art, Music and Drama can also be quite tricky because they require creativity and aesthetic sensitivity. Science, Maths and ICT are often strong subjects.

Although it's good to get lots of qualifications, if an aspie is really struggling with certain subjects and becoming overwhelmed, it may be better to drop them and concentrate on taking fewer subjects, but getting better grades. Of course it's very important to get advice from teachers, as some subjects, such as Maths, Science and English, are widely accepted by employers and colleges as being more important than others. I would always recommend maintaining *at the very least* five GCSE subjects, including Maths and English. It is also important to remember that employers and educational institutions tend to only focus on your highest level qualifications. College only looks at GCSEs, university focuses on A levels, and I am now in the situation where when applying for doctorate courses, my A levels are pretty useless, when once they were the most important thing in the world!

Some schools also offer other qualifications that give you training and experience in a particular field of work. This kind of vocational qualification often appeals to people with AS because they can see how it will lead to a job or career, whereas they don't see the point in studying some academic subjects. It can also offer the chance for aspies who are not academic to develop other skills and strengths, which will give them a sense of achievement and self-respect.

PREPARING FOR EXAMS

Preparing for exams often involves lots of revision. The problem with revision is that it is often quite boring, and it has no immediate end product. The teacher may set revision for homework but he or she is not going to know whether you have actually done it or not. The temptation is to avoid doing it, particularly as it often seems like a huge task and you don't know where to start. It really helps if you get to grips with revision early on. You need to have a plan and stick to it. Once you are in a routine, it becomes easier to keep going. Work out how much time you have before the exams start, and how many subjects you have to revise for. Schedule a set time in each week to revise each subject. Even now, when I revise for university exams, I set out a schedule for the coming month of what I am going to revise and when. There are various things that can help with revision. There are study guides which contain all the important stuff for a particular subject. A copy of the exam syllabus gives you a clear idea about what areas of the subject are important. Working through past papers can be very helpful, because you get a better understanding of the kind of answers the examiners are looking for. Past papers also highlight the gaps in your knowledge, so you know what you need to work on.

Some people find they can revise by just reading through all the material, but the problem with this is that people often find that they are reading the information without really taking it in. It can help to try to pick out the important points and write them down as you go along, perhaps on a postcard. You end up with a set of postcards on a particular subject which will remind you of what is important. You can even put them together and use them to create a mind map of the whole subject. A mind map is a chart where you see how the different parts of a subject link together, which gives you an overview of the whole subject. In many subjects there are also things that just have to be memorised, such as dates or formulas or quotes. Again, write them down on postcards and work through them, memorising each one, and then test yourself on them regularly. However, this requires good writing and drawing ability, and helps if you are a visual learner. Some of us do not fit that model. Some learn better by trying to teach it to other people, or doing demos. I learn best by lecturing myself on a subject. Revision is a very personal thing, and needs to be done on an individual basis.

All this is an ideal to aim for. Some aspies are very good at working on their own and being conscientious. Other aspies find it difficult to focus on academic work because they find just getting through a normal school day quite taxing. I remember trying to revise for my GCSEs after my breakdown. It seemed like an impossible task because I had taken very little in during my time at school. Most of the time I had been in a state of turmoil inside, though outwardly seeming to cope. I did what I could in order to revise, which wasn't very much, and I didn't achieve good results. When I moved to the right environment, and when I knew what I wanted to do with my life, it became much easier. It's important to find a balance between pushing yourself to achieve your potential and recognising when you might need to make some allowances for your temperament and your state of mind.

People with AS vary in how well they respond to the pressure of working for exams. Some aspies take the whole thing almost too seriously and become overwhelmed by the importance of the exams and how much they need to do. If an aspie is getting too stressed about the exam issue, it can help to be able to ignore it all for a few hours and do something completely different that takes their mind off of exams. It can also be useful to talk about what would actually happen if they didn't achieve the results they hoped for. Sometimes an aspie can expect this to be a catastrophe that doesn't bear thinking about. But it's usually possible to resit exams, so the situation is rarely irretrievable.

At the opposite extreme, there are some aspies who simply don't care about the exams. In this case, there are two ways to tackle it. You can reason with them to try to make them see why the exams are important. You can talk through the ways in which failing exams might affect their plans for the future, as sometimes we cannot see the knock-on effects. However, sometimes this simply doesn't register. They may not have any plans for the future and find the prospect difficult to imagine. Alternatively, they may just decide they don't want to listen, in which case whatever you say will be redundant. In this case you may need to try a bit of bribery and blackmail. DVDs, computer games, chocolates, sweets, or even money can be used as a reward for revision or good scores. All aspies have their weaknesses for the little pleasures in life, and mum and dad are likely to know what these are. Failing to do any revision can result in the temporary loss of a favourite pastime, such as the use of the TV or computer. This is fair if you have explained that this will be the consequence for a complete lack of effort, and if your expectations are reasonable. In the end you cannot force someone to work, and getting into a battle of wills can be counterproductive. Often revision time is included within lessons when exams are approaching, so even if little revision is done at home, there will be some revision at school.

Most aspies fall somewhere between these two extremes of taking the exams too seriously and becoming stressed, and ignoring the approach of exams in the hope that they will go away. Often the dilemma is knowing if and when a bit of parental intervention is needed, either to calm frazzled nerves or to encourage a bit more effort.

EXAM CONCESSIONS

Exam concessions are simply ways of adapting exams to make it a fairer playing field for everyone. For example, if someone is quite slow at reading and/or writing they may need to have extra time to finish an exam. Applying for concessions can be a lengthy process, so it needs to be begun months in advance. The following is a list of the most useful concessions.

- *Extra time* – normally an additional 25 per cent of the allocated time for an exam.

- *Use of a computer* – for students whose handwriting is difficult to read. The computer is not connected to the internet, so only the word processing facility is available.

- *Use of a scribe* – an alternative for students with handwriting problems. However, dictating your answers to another person can feel awkward for a person with AS. It may be better to opt for using the computer, and to work on your typing skills before the exams.

- *Use of a reader* – for students who have a problem with reading, for example, those who are quite dyslexic. This person is there to read the exam questions to the candidate. If a scribe is also needed, the same person does both jobs.

- *Use of a transcriber* – another alternative for students with handwriting problems. The students write the answers themselves, but when the exam is finished the transcribers copy out the answers neatly.

- *Use of a private room* – this is a concession that I highly recommend for aspies. The candidate is in a room on their own apart from the invigilator. This reduces the sensory distractions and can feel less intimidating than being in a big hall with dozens of other candidates. If the person has any repetitive behaviour that they find themselves doing when concentrating, such as leg jiggling, it can be a relief not to worry about distracting other candidates. The invigilator may sometimes be a bit more flexible. For example, if both student and invigilator happen to arrive a bit early, they may start the exam slightly early, which means less waiting around getting nervous. Or if the candidate is already very nervous, the invigilator may start the exam slightly later to give them time to calm down and collect themselves. However, this is at the invigilator's discretion, so don't assume that this will happen.

If a student needs one or more of these concessions it's obviously important to apply for it. Don't assume that the school will realise a concession is necessary for a particular student. It may be up to parents to raise the issue with the school, and this needs to be done well in advance of the actual exams.

EXAM DAYS

Exam days can be quite stressful. Often there are now several exams in each subject, which may be spread throughout the course of the two years. This is better than the old system of having all the exams at the end, as it spreads the pressure. Also, students get a mark for each exam, which gives them a clear idea of whether they are putting in enough work. The disadvantage is that there are lots of exams, and there are always exams looming ahead.

On the days of the exams it's best if parents remain calm and upbeat. There are often things that need to be taken to exams, such as equipment and possibly ID cards and entry forms. If parents make sure that their children have everything they need (preferably checked the day before to prevent last minute panic) it can help relieve some of the stress. If the aspie usually travels by public transport to get to school, it may be better to take them by car, if possible. This avoids the possibility of delays and cancellations causing them to arrive late and in a panic. However, for some aspies any fussing or special treatment just makes things worse. They prefer things to be kept as normal as possible.

EXAM RESULTS

Most people get a bit anxious at the end of the two years when the time approaches for getting their final grades. This is particularly true if the grades they get are going to materially affect their future plans. It's a good idea to have talked through the possibilities in advance, so that you have a plan in place if, for example, the results are not what was hoped for. It's important not to get into the situation where aspies feel they have ruined their whole life because of a bad exam result. On the other hand, a few aspies may just need the reality check of a disappointing result in order to see that a complete lack of effort has consequences. In the end, whether the exam results are a cause for celebration, commiseration or even recrimination, the ultimate message to convey is that you believe in your son or daughter and recognise their potential. They *can* build themselves a good life and a good future if they have a realistic idea of what they want and are willing to work at it.

YOUNG ADULTS

Many new options open up at 16. It may be possible to go out and get a job. There are courses which train you in specific work skills, for example GNVQs, diplomas and NVQs. They often provide a good mix of education and practical experience. Many colleges will have courses to suit a whole range of abilities including people who have a learning disability, so it's worth researching what is available. Some aspies opt to do A levels, and many find they actually prefer this to studying for GCSEs, because they are able to specialise in their best subjects even more so than at GCSE.

Before making any decisions about what to do at 16 it's important to get advice and do research, and this needs to be done early because the process of applying can be lengthy. Careers advisers have a good knowledge of which qualifications to aim for if there is already a career in mind. Even if aspies have no idea about what they want to do in the future, advisers may be able to suggest things they hadn't thought of, and can also give advice about which qualifications enable them to keep options open, if opting for further study. It's also important to visit colleges to get a more realistic idea of what they are like.

There may be a choice between school sixth form and further education college, though many vocational courses are available only in colleges. For me, college was a lot nicer than secondary school. I was able to start afresh with new people who didn't have any preconceptions about me. If you had a bad experience at school, there are a lot of advantages in leaving it all behind. However, some aspies find the size of the college and the mix of students a bit overwhelming. They prefer sticking with what they know by staying at school – for them the devil you know beats the devil you don't. This allows them to focus on their studies rather than having to cope with a whole new social scene. At both college and in the sixth form at school, the students are usually there because they want be, which makes for a good working environment. This avoids the problem of having students in the class who are not interested in learning and tend to be disruptive.

Usually when students apply to a college, they are expected to attend an interview. People with AS sometimes interview very well because they don't feel the social pressure of the interview. Others interview less well, either because they do feel the pressure, or because they don't see what relevance the interview is to their ability to do well on the course. It's worth doing a bit of interview preparation beforehand. The questions usually focus around what you want to study, why you want to study it and why you want to go to this particular college. It helps to have thought through good answers, and to also be prepared to talk about hobbies and interests. It is also useful to role-play interviews. Someone with AS may not realise that the interviewer may offer them a handshake when they walk into the room. The person with AS may look down and mumble when they answer questions, or they may talk at great length. They may not be aware that the interviewer will probably ask them if they have any questions, or that it gives a good impression if they have a couple of suitable questions prepared. A bit of practice can help to iron out these kind of problems, and make the real interview much easier.

It really helps if the college understands Asperger syndrome and is willing to take AS needs seriously. Colleges should have a SENCO and it's important to make sure they understand the particular needs of the person with AS. It helps if the college has had students with AS before, but even then staff at the college may assume that they know what is needed, when in reality each person with AS is different. The ideal would be to have the college put the details of the way in which your child will be supported in writing.

Often it is the small things that can make a difference to how well someone adjusts to life at college. For example, it may be enough for most students to just be told when to turn up on the first day, but some people with AS may find the lack of information about exactly where to go and what to do causes a lot of anxiety, even to the point of not wanting to go in at all. Having basic details beforehand, such as the layout of the college, what to do at lunch time, and the timings of the college day can help an aspie feel less overwhelmed with new information on the first day. It also helps to have identified a place to go if in need of some peace and quiet (often the library is a good option), and a person and place to go to if in need of help.

The relationship between staff and students is often different in college. Teachers might use their first names and the classes may be relatively small. A teacher will often see a particular class several times a week. This can work to the advantage of students with AS because the teacher knows each student quite well. Once the student with AS gets to know and trust a teacher, they may feel confident enough to talk to the teacher personally and explain what they find hard, why it is hard, and what would help them. The teacher may be interested enough to want to find out more about Asperger syndrome, in which case you could always lend them this book!

COURSEWORK FOR A LEVELS

There is a big difference between studying for GCSEs and A levels. Often the lessons involve listening to the teacher or lecturer talk about a particular topic, and making notes. It is quite difficult for most people to listen and take notes at the same time, and is even more difficult for someone with AS. Sometimes the learning support department is able to provide an assistant to take notes. The teachers may be willing to make photocopies of their own notes and give them to the student. Alternatively the learning support department might hire a student in the same class to make notes and then give photocopies to the student with AS. However, it may not be possible to get this level of support. Another option is to record the lectures and make notes afterwards, though this is quite time consuming. If the aspie is good at touch typing, the most practical solution may be to use a laptop for taking notes.

In post-16 education the students are generally expected to take responsibility for their own progress. At the start students sometimes think that college is really easy because there are lots of gaps in the timetable where there are no lessons. Often they don't realise that they need to use at least some of the free time to work on assignments and go over anything in the lessons they didn't understand. It's also tempting to skip a lesson occasionally, or to not do an assignment, because there aren't the same kind of penalties for this as there were at school. However, at this level the teachers have to get a lot of information across in each lesson, and they set assignments that help the student assimilate what they have been taught. It's very easy to fall behind and miss important work if you don't take the whole process seriously right from the start.

THINKING ABOUT UNIVERSITY

Some people will plan to get a job after completing college or sixth form, others will want to continue their training or education. For students doing A level courses there is the option of going to university. Many aspies welcome the opportunity to study their favourite subject at an advanced level, and do very well.

University is very different from school or college. It requires much more self-sufficiency in many different areas. For the first time you have to be responsible for looking after yourself. You have to make sure your clothes are reasonably clean, your room is in a liveable state, and that you don't run out of hygiene essentials such as toothpaste and deodorant. You also need to manage your money. This means that there is a lot to keep track of, in addition to the academic pressures. However, I have found university to be a very accepting environment, and I know this is a view shared by others. Universities are quite enlightened about supporting students with special needs and the student union can be another source of help and advice. It can all seem daunting at first but it is possible for aspies to survive and thrive, particularly if they are able to access the support available.

Choosing a university needs to be done with great care. Once a subject has been decided on it's a good idea to look at some university league tables to see which universities do well in that subject. Once you have some idea of the grades you may achieve at A level you can gauge which universities are possible choices.

It's then important to consider other factors about the different universities. The environment needs to be right. For example, I would not be able to tolerate the stress of an inner city university like London; I needed somewhere quiet and peaceful, somewhere where I could 'get away from it all'. It's well worth actually visiting the different universities, as this gives you a much clearer idea of what it would be like to live there. Most universities have open days. This also gives you a chance to see the halls of residence, at least from the outside. It's worth researching the types of accommodation the university offers. Some halls have shared rooms, some provide most meals, and some expect the students to self-cater to a large extent. Some halls have rooms with their own small bathroom, others don't. Many universities only have accommodation for first years, though they may make exceptions for people with a recognised special need. It's also useful to see where the halls are located, their proximity to other university buildings and the availability of local facilities such as shops.

This kind of research is particularly important for people with AS because it is often difficult for us to imagine what life at university will be like. Actually going to visit a particular university gives us a better idea of this. Seeing several different universities brings out the contrast between them, otherwise it's easy to assume that they are all roughly the same. There may be one that particularly stands out as a place where you would want to spend three years.

Another reason why research is important to aspies is that we tend to be less flexible about what we can and cannot tolerate. Many of us would hate to share a room. Sharing facilities may also be a problem. For example, a shared kitchen can often get quite dirty, it tends to involve a certain amount of turn-taking and negotiation about using the equipment, and people sometimes 'borrow' your food. This could be very stressful and/or annoying for someone with AS. It's also possible that the aspie might unwittingly annoy other people by trying to insist that things are done a particular way.

Generally the best option for aspies just starting at university is to choose catered accommodation in a hall of residence. I know in my first year there was so much going on, there was no way I would have been able to cope with the work *and* cooking for myself every night. I would recommend getting a single room if at all possible, preferably with its own shower room.

DISABLED STUDENTS ALLOWANCE

Some students with Asperger syndrome may qualify for the Disabled Students Allowance (DSA). This has various elements, but includes specialist equipment. For example, if you have a significant difficulty in taking legible notes it may be possible to get a laptop to write with, or a dictaphone on which to record lectures. If you have problems with self-organisation, it might be possible to get a personal organiser. In some cases a non-medical helper may be provided who can check that you are coping and looking after yourself. It's worth finding out the details of DSA well in advance of starting university, in case you do qualify, because the application process is quite involved.

UNIVERSITY LIFE

However well you try to prepare for university life, it's always a steep learning curve, even for neurotypicals. One thing that seems to help the settling in process is to have contact with someone who has already completed a year or two at the university. Some of the older universities have an 'academic family' system where two experienced students look after a new student. I would certainly not be doing nearly as well at university if it was not for Hatty and Phil, my academic parents. They really helped me settle in, and learn the ropes. It may be that friends of parents have a son or daughter at the university, or they might know someone who does. Or your school or college may know of former pupils who are there. This person might be willing to have a chat with you about university life before you actually start there. Most people who have been at university for a while are very positive and enthusiastic about university life. The knowledge that eventually university can be really good can sometimes sustain you through any bad patches at the beginning when you might wonder why you ever thought university was a good idea. This person might even be willing to show you around once you start at university, and occasionally meet up for a coffee. Of course, if the other person is very different from you, this might not be useful, but sometimes it can work well. Just having occasional contact with someone who understands what it's like to have to get a big assignment in on time, or to be woken up at 2 o'clock in the morning because some joker has set off the fire alarm in your hall or residence *again*, is quite reassuring. However, many people will not have the good fortune of already knowing someone before they start at university.

Most universities start with 'Freshers' Week'. This is a special week for new students who are just settling in, where there are lots of events and students can join any of the societies or clubs that are run by students. Unfortunately this week is essentially one big party – and many aspies don't 'do' parties. There will probably also be some quieter events which may be more appealing. If you have a particular interest it's a good idea to join the relevant society because it gives you contact with like-minded people. I joined the Ents Crew, who are responsible for setting up and running all the sound and lighting equipment for university entertainment events. I had no particular interest in this but it was suggested by my excellent academic mum, who was part of the Ents Crew. In some ways it seems like a really bad choice for an aspie because when an event is happening the music is *very* loud, there are loads of people, and bright lights. However, it's often easier for an aspie to work on a task with other people rather than standing around socialising, and people really appreciate that you turn up and are willing to help. So, even if there is no society for your particular interest, it could be worth joining one which involves you in working together with other students. There is often a good sense of camaraderie, and it gives you a break from studying.

Relaxation and the opportunity to unwind are very important, particularly in the first term when everything is new and there is so much to think about. I find a TV and DVDs are essential, for other people it might be video games or books or music. It's important to be able to enjoy spending time on your own, and most aspies are quite good at this. These things can stop you feeling lost and lonely when you come back each day to an empty room. When you've done your work you can reward yourself with a bit of 'me time', watching a DVD or playing a video game.

A computer is probably a necessity for work, but is also an important means of keeping in touch with friends and family. A mobile phone is another essential, particularly if you have a list of useful numbers that you might need for various eventualities. It gives a sense of security and the knowledge that you are not really alone, even if you only need to phone home to ask how to operate a tumble drier. If you get into a fix, you will have the phone numbers you need.

Lots of aspies don't need a lot of social contact, but there are drawbacks in becoming too isolated. If you become known as 'the guy who never talks to anyone', it can be quite difficult to break free of that image. The longer you go without talking to anyone, the harder it becomes to do it. You don't need to talk to everyone: there may be lots of people you never speak with, as long as there are a few people you occasionally chat to, however briefly. The secret seems to be to find some like-minded people, which is why it's useful to join some kind of society. Or there may be like-minded people studying the same subject as you, particularly if you are studying something quite technical. Sometimes it can seem as if everyone else at university is always partying and you are the only one who isn't interested in this. There will be other people like you; they just aren't as noisy as the party people.

It's very important to establish a good balance between work and relaxation at university, and relaxation should include a few activities which get you out of your room, preferably with some other people. If you are constantly working and rarely having contact with other people, it becomes a bit of a 'pressure-cooker' existence. Small problems can become large problems in your head because you never get a break from your own concerns. Just getting out and doing something different allows you to focus on something else and come back refreshed.

If you do begin to get into difficulties, whether they be academic, financial or just getting stressed out and miserable, it's important to get a bit of help and advice. It's much better to get help early on rather than letting things progress and get worse. Most problems can be sorted out, or at least eased, if they are caught early enough. You definitely don't want things to get so bad that you can see no solution. There is no shame in asking for help when you need it, in fact it's the most sensible thing to do. Most universities have a student advisory service or a welfare service, or some kind of helpline. A bit of searching on the internet will probably give you the relevant information. Each university also has its own disability advisory service, which can be very helpful, though not all aspies have a diagnosis. The Student Support Service at St Andrews was particularly good. They contacted me before my A level results to talk about what support I would like, and how to best deliver it. They also talked about university life, and made me feel more confident about the process. In addition, I have meetings with my support adviser every semester (although I can have more if I wish) to make sure things are going okay.

It can be difficult to adjust to university life, but it's possible to get through the bad bits. It can be very satisfying to have managed to become independent and to begin to forge a life of your own. But everyone's experience is different, so if in the end you find university is not right for you, it's always possible to find another way forward.

8

BULLYING

When Being Different isn't Cool

One of the most unpleasant aspects of school is bullying. As adults we can choose who we spend time with, at least to some extent, but children are stuck with whoever happens to be in their class. Even if their classmates change, it seems there are always a few who will enjoy annoying and upsetting other people. However, in recent years there has been a far greater recognition of the problem. Schools are now required to have an anti-bullying policy. This hasn't remedied the situation but at least schools will now have thought through their attitude to bullying and the way they deal with it.

Kidscape has done a huge amount of work in this area and on its website there is a sample Anti-Bullying Policy for Schools, which gives a clear idea of what an anti-bullying policy would include. It begins with a statement of intent, which says:

> We are committed to providing a caring, friendly and safe environment for all our pupils so they can learn in a relaxed and secure atmosphere. Bullying of any kind is unacceptable at our school. If bullying does occur, all pupils should be able to tell and know that incidents will be dealt with promptly and effectively. (Kidscape 2005, p.2)

This statement makes me want to cheer. The policy also emphasises that no one deserves to be bullied and everyone should be treated with respect. It is clear in the policy that the school has a responsibility to deal with incidents of bullying.

A school policy doesn't prevent bullying because it still happens a lot. But at least the intentions are good and the attitude to bullying is proactive. Previously there may have been a tendency to view bullying as just an unfortunate part of the way pupils behaved with each other, which wasn't the school's responsibility unless it occurred right in front of the teacher. There may also have been an attitude that it could be partly a child's own fault if they were bullied, either because they were in some way different from everybody else, or because they should learn how to take a joke or just learn to stick up for themselves.

It should be possible to find out what the anti-bullying policy of your child's school is. Secondary schools are more likely to have a detailed document, probably because in primary schools the teachers have far more contact with their own classes, and so are in a better position to deal flexibly with any bullying issues that arise.

A detailed anti-bullying policy should have a statement of intent, which describes the school's attitude to bullying and the kind of environment the school is aiming to create. It should also have a comprehensive list of types of bullying, such as name-calling, threats, physically hurting another pupil, and so on. This list is very helpful if you are unsure whether a particular act counts as bullying. It will also describe signs and symptoms that a child is being bullied, the procedure to be followed when bullying is reported, and the range of possible consequences for the bully. It will also outline preventative measures, such as educating the pupils to report any bullying they see happening.

A clear policy helps teachers because it enables them to act effectively and with confidence. Whereas before they might have been unsure about whether a particular behaviour counted as bullying or not, and unsure what their response ought to be, now they know exactly what the school expects. It also gives children and parents confidence that any complaints of bullying will be taken seriously.

ASPERGER SYNDROME AND BULLYING

Unfortunately children with AS can be particularly vulnerable to bullying. Some children with AS are obviously 'different' and this makes them a target. Perhaps they have coordination problems and so walk in an odd way, or they may have mannerisms that mark them out. Other aspies may be quite naive, so other kids like playing tricks on them. Some have a short temper so other children enjoy 'setting them off' by causing them to lose their temper at inappropriate times. Quite a few aspies have a tendency to get quite stressed and anxious, and this can make them vulnerable. If someone starts teasing or goading an aspie, the aspie often lacks the verbal facility to come back at them with a smart retort. It's probably true that most people have had experiences of being teased or bullied at some point in their school life, but those with AS tend to get more than their fair share.

One of the problems with bullying is that it can take many different forms. The obvious example is one boy deliberately targeting another. The bully sets out to make the other boy's life miserable. He will make nasty remarks, call names, maybe physically hurt the other boy, perhaps hide his belongings, anything he can think of to make his victim suffer. Often he will get his friends to join in, and will even try to scare off the victim's friends so that he is quite isolated. The boy doing the bullying may have a grudge against his chosen victim, but it may be for no reason at all. This is a horrible situation. The victim feels vulnerable all the time because he never knows when the bully will strike, or what the bully will do next.

Often bullying is more casual and general than this. One person might tend to be treated unkindly and unfairly by lots of different people. They might occasionally make jokes about him, ignore or exclude him, elbow him out of the way when queuing for lunch, or just generally treat him with contempt. These people are not deliberately targeting this person and might be surprised and resentful if their behaviour was described as bullying. However, over time it can seriously undermine the victim's confidence and self-respect. There is usually nothing about this person that 'deserves' this kind of treatment. In fact often the people who are picked on in this way are nice kids who just want to get through the school day without any social hassles. If they have AS they are less able to deflect and defuse this kind of negative attention. They are therefore an easy target. The person with AS can end up feeling powerless in the face of this kind of casual meanness.

Often an aspie will respond in one of two ways. Some become more and more angry inside until one day they 'flip' and completely lose their temper. It can be over some relatively minor slight, but to the aspie, this is just one insult too many. However, to other people this response seems quite unreasonable, and it's the aspie who ends up in trouble. Another aspie response is to lose confidence and become more and more withdrawn.

Sometimes the only people who see how much of an impact the ill-treatment is having are the parents. If children suddenly become more angry and aggressive at home it can be a sign that they are being bullied. It's not safe for them to get angry at school because it will make things worse or get them into trouble with the teachers. The only safe place to vent their feelings is at home. Another reaction is to start treating younger siblings badly because the child is copying the treatment they are getting at school. If a child seems withdrawn, gets upset easily, and doesn't seem to want to do things they previously enjoyed, this is a sign of depression and may indicate that they are being 'picked on' at school.

Quite often children who are having social problems at school won't be keen to go out when they are at home. They may be worried about accidentally seeing other children from school while out and about. This can be particularly true at secondary school age, because it's quite possible that there will be other students in local popular spots such as the shopping centre or the cinema. When I was being bullied I wouldn't even go to the shop, which was five minutes' walk from my home, just in case I came across people from school. The only place I really felt safe and could relax was at home.

One of the worst aspects of being bullied is that it can badly affect a child's view of himself. Whereas previously he may have been happily getting on with life, though with the usual ups and downs, now he may start to question himself. If other pupils at school treat him with contempt he may start to think that he must be somehow a contemptible person. He will start to assume that the reason he is being picked on must be because of some fundamental inadequacy within himself, believing that if only he was different – more popular, or tougher, or better at sports, or just somehow a better as a person – he wouldn't be treated like this. This is horrible because not only is life miserable but also he feels that he has somehow brought this treatment on himself by being failing to be the kind of person other people expect him to be. He may even start to despise himself and become very angry or depressed about just being who he is.

It can also affect a child's view of other people and life in general. The child may start to believe that no one can be trusted and that they are all out to get him. He may become very guarded because he thinks that if he shows any weakness or makes any mistakes people will immediately seize on the opportunity to make him look stupid. It makes it hard to take a risk and try anything new.

People with AS tend to be particularly vulnerable to the personal impact of bullying for two reasons. First, our self-confidence tends to be more shaky. We can sense that we are not the same as most other people and we have to work at keeping hold of the belief that we are just as good as everyone else. This belief can be completely undermined by being bullied and picked on, especially if we are being called a weirdo or a freak. I strongly believe that aspies have a valuable contribution to make in any setting, *because* we are different and have a unique perspective. It makes me angry when young aspies completely lose confidence because they are treated with derision by people who assume their own superiority.

The second reason is that we are more vulnerable to the impact of bullying is that we tend to be more rigid in our thinking. We have to find rules to live by because otherwise life seems complicated and bewildering. We haven't the kind of social awareness which guides the way most people make sense of the things that happen to them. If we decide it's not safe to trust other people, because they will take advantage of us and make us look foolish, it's quite difficult for us to change that. We automatically notice things that confirm the rule, and discount things that contradict it. We interpret everything that happens to us in the light of that rule, so maybe we think people are trying to trick us or mock us even when that was not their intention. When my brother Jack was being laughed at in school by a couple of boys who were more able than him, he didn't want to go out of the house, because if he happened to see people in the street who were laughing and smiling together, he was sure they were laughing at him, even though they didn't even know him.

PRIMARY SCHOOL

If you begin to suspect that your child is being bullied, it's important to speak to the teacher to let him or her know of your concerns. However, it is sometimes difficult with children who have AS to find out exactly what has been going on. Often they come home and just want to forget about the school day. The first sign you have that there is a problem may be your child coming home very angry and upset. This might actually be the culmination of lots of little incidents of bullying that have been happening over time. Alternatively your child may be becoming more and more reluctant to go to school.

It's important to try to get an accurate account of what's been happening. This can be problematic because sometimes people with AS are not good at explaining this kind of thing clearly. It involves being able to pick out which events were important and putting them in the right order. It's worth being patient, listening carefully and asking questions. If your child is upset, you may need to wait until later to find out the details.

Sometimes aspies are not very clear about what is and what is not bullying. For example, there may be someone at school who they don't get on with, who makes nasty comments, and who doesn't let them join in with the games in the playground. This isn't necessarily bullying, though it can be. Bullying is a matter of the other person's intentions. If they are deliberately victimising someone and this is sustained over time, it's bullying. Aspies aren't very good working out other people's intentions. It may even be that they are being bullied, or at least taken advantage of, and they don't realise it.

If you begin to suspect your child is being bullied, it's important to speak to the teacher. It can also help to keep a note of each incident that happens as this will give the teacher a much clearer idea of what is going on. Try to keep your record factual. For example, it's better to write down, 'James stopped my son from joining in a game they were all playing at break time, and called him a stupid idiot,' rather than, 'James bullied my son at playtime and called him names.' If the problem is not that your child is being bullied by one particular child, but is being treated unkindly by several people, it's equally important to make a note of any examples of this, again so that the teacher can get an accurate account of what is happening.

Another important aspect of talking to your child is to give them a helpful perspective on what happened. Children who are being bullied often begin to think that it must be because there is something wrong about them that causes people to do this. You need to give them the message that everyone has a right to be treated decently. They need to see that actually the fault is not with them but with the person or people doing the bullying.

One of the best things about primary schools is that the teachers know the children in their class well. They spend lots of time with the children and so have much more influence on the way they behave towards each other than do teachers in secondary schools. Once the teacher has been alerted to the problem, she or he will become much more aware of when it might be happening. The teacher can intervene in various ways, and will probably talk to the children involved in bullying, but may also steer your child towards more positive friendships. The school's anti-bullying policy should explain what happens in cases of bullying.

Once you have consulted the teacher about a bullying problem, it's really important to keep an accurate record of any further incidents which you can show the teacher if the situation is not improving. It's much easier for teachers to intervene if they are confident they know what's been happening. Sometimes the teacher will suggest that your child tells him or her if any more problems with bullying occur. However, this can be difficult for some children with AS. It can be hard to find a suitable moment to tell the teacher, as teachers are busy people, and it is also often difficult for someone with AS to explain things clearly and in the right order, especially if they are upset and angry. So, while ideally the child should be able to talk to the teacher when problems occur, it may be easier for an aspie to talk to parents at home.

The teacher should be able to deal effectively with bullying, but if there are situations which always seem to cause trouble, it may be best to provide the aspie with an alternative. For example, if an aspie ends up wandering around on his own in the playground because nobody wants him to join in their games, it's better to allow him to go to the library or to a room where he could spend break time doing Lego or some other pastime. If lunch time is always a problem because he doesn't have anyone to sit with, perhaps a place can be saved for him near a friendly adult. These measures can help if the child hates playtime or lunch time because they are always difficult.

It's very important to keep communicating with the school if the problems continue. In the Kidscape sample Anti-Bullying Policy for Schools, the importance of a good working relationship between teachers and parents when dealing with bullying is emphasised (Kidscape 2005). If you are still concerned you need to tell the teacher. The school should be monitoring the situation, but teachers may not have realised that the problem is still there or has returned.

Very occasionally things seem to break down irretrievably, despite everyone's best efforts over an extended time. If your child has begun to hate school and is very distressed by the whole situation, it can sometimes be best to look for a new school. This clearly is not a step to be taken lightly, and is very much a last resort, once all possible strategies have been tried. But if your child is being completely ground down by the situation to the extent that you fear that it may be doing lasting damage to their well-being, it just might be the best thing to do, particularly if there is another school where your child does have a friend.

STRATEGIES FOR TEACHERS

There are various strategies teachers can use which have been shown to reduce bullying in primary schools. Some of these involve getting children to think and talk about the issue of bullying. This can help them to be clear in their own minds about exactly what bullying is. It also helps if they are encouraged to talk about what it might feel like to be bullied, so they understand the personal impact that this has. They may then be able to come up with ideas on what to do if someone is being bullied. For example, they can talk about what to do if they see someone being bullied (tell the teacher). If children come up with ideas themselves they often feel more inclined to put them into practice.

Circle time is often used as an opportunity to talk about these kind of issues. In circle time the class and teacher sit round in a circle. Sometimes they play games or do a fun activity, and sometimes they have a discussion. The idea is that the children are encouraged to listen to each other and respect each other's views. This way they feel confident about contributing. There is a relaxed, positive atmosphere where the contribution of each child is valued. The teacher can use this time to have a discussion about bullying; what bullying is, what it feels like to be bullied, and ways of helping people who are being bullied. Often when children think about these issues they are more inclined to act in a kinder way.

Team-building exercises can also help children to work cooperatively with each other. This involves the children assigning tasks, helping each other and sharing information. Often this can begin to generate new friendships among children. A child who is often socially isolated can mix with other children in a new context. Other children may see this child in a different way, because they become more aware of the positive contribution he or she can make.

Befriending can also help, particularly if it is done by a group of children rather than just one child, though that, too, can work. It may be that the teacher would need to talk to the group of children to see if they would be willing to include the isolated child (social isolation is recognised as a form of bullying). If they raise objections, the teacher can have a discussion with them about this too. For example, it may be that they say this child gets angry really quickly, or that he doesn't say much. This opens the way to talking about what they could do if he got angry, or how they could help him to talk a bit more. When children are asked for their views and ideas about a particular task, such as befriending a particular child, they are more inclined to take responsibility for it and to try to make it work. They feel that what they are doing is valued and respected by the teacher. However, the good intentions of children don't last very long unless they are regularly supported and reinforced by the teacher.

Another approach is for the teacher to chat to each of the children involved in the bullying privately to encourage each of them to consider how their behaviour is making the bullied child feel. The idea is to get the children doing the bullying to acknowledge that it must be making him unhappy. The children can then be asked if they can suggest any ways of avoiding making him unhappy. The children may need prompting about the kind of thing that might help, such as being friendly, not teasing, as so on. The bullied child is then spoken to individually to explain what has happened and the ideas suggested. If there are some behaviours of his which tended to result in negative attention, such as annoying behaviours or getting angry really easily, these can be discussed to see how they can be avoided. However, it's important to emphasise that this doesn't mean he deserved to be bullied. Again, it's important to follow up with the individual children a week or so later, to see how well things are going.

SECONDARY SCHOOL

Primary school and secondary school are very different environments. Pupils are more vulnerable to bullying in secondary school because there is much less supervision during break times and the times when they are walking from one lesson to the next. There is often a lot of laddish behaviour from the boys. It seems important to many of them to show off a bit and look big. Part of this is done by making jokes about other pupils, annoying other pupils or doing things like casually shoving them out of the way. These boys tend to get bored during the lessons and needling another pupil can be an entertaining diversion. Aspies can get more than their fair share of this kind of treatment for various reasons. A lot of aspies tend to get stressed quite easily, which makes them an easy target. Some are easily provoked into angry outbursts, and some are naive and easily tricked. Children who are quiet are seen as being less likely to retaliate, and those who do not have many friends don't have a group who might stick up for them.

I remember one incident that illustrates all of this. Lots of classes were assembled in the school hall, listening in hushed silence while the headmaster said his piece. Some boys near me indicated that they wanted to look at my watch, so, not wanting to appear unfriendly, I undid it and passed it to them. When they had finished admiring it, they passed it back. A minute or two later my watch started bleeping its alarm. Everyone turned to see who was making this noise, while I struggled frantically to turn it off, much to the amusement of the boys who had, of course, set the alarm. I was naive, I got very stressed about the whole thing. If I was the kind of aspie who gets angry rather than anxious, I probably would have yelled at them and got into trouble for disrupting the headmaster's talk. For those boys it was just a harmless prank on some idiot who should have known better. It gave them a laugh, relieved the boredom and was soon forgotten. For me it was a mortifying incident which still brings me out in a cold sweat when I think about it.

At secondary school age, children become more able to be manipulative. This can mean that some pupils will take advantage of other kids. For example, one pupil may make friends with another and then ask for lots of favours, such as lending money for lunch (which isn't ever paid back), or copying homework answers. It can be hard for aspies to realise when they are being used in this way. Often the other pupil will say something like, 'Could you just lend me some money for lunch, because we're friends, aren't we.' If the aspie doesn't have many other friends they may feel they have to keep giving in, just to preserve the friendship. It's not unknown for a manipulator to subtly put off other kids who might want to be friends with the aspie, so that the aspie is even more dependent on the one friendship. More common is a situation where one pupil will act friendly just because the aspie has something he wants, and then ignore the aspie as soon as he has got it. Often this works partly because the aspie is a bit intimidated by the other child.

Naive aspies are particularly vulnerable to exploitation. They have very little insight into the motives of other people and tend to take whatever they are told as being true. Other kids often get the aspie to do things or say things which they know will get him into trouble, because it amuses them. For example, they will get the aspie to ask the teacher a very inappropriate question, or to write something really rude on the blackboard (or whiteboard). The aspie may realise that what they are doing is slightly dodgy, but think they are all sharing in the joke, and that these people are his friends. The aspie may be totally taken aback by the outraged reaction of the teacher. More sinister is the involvement of the aspie in things that are actively wrong, such as shoplifting. If the aspie is told, 'Don't tell anyone, this is our secret,' the aspie will keep quiet, which can mean that the exploitation continues.

One of the good things about secondary school nowadays is that they normally have a detailed, formalised anti-bullying policy, which was probably not the case when I was at school a few years ago. This should contain a definition of the kind of behaviour the school regards as bullying, their aims and objectives in dealing with this (for example, to provide a school environment where every pupil can work without fear), the procedures which should be followed if an incident of bullying occurs and the kind of sanctions that might be implemented. It should be possible to get a copy of the school's anti-bullying policy, or to access this online.

At secondary school age it's particularly important to try to keep the channels of communication with your child open. Aspies are often not good communicators, and may want to just forget about school when they are at home. At this age boys often become even less chatty and may want to give the impression that they can handle whatever problems may arise. Sometimes they think it is somehow a bit cowardly to tell parents or teachers something which would get another child into trouble, and this can be exploited by bullies. An aspie can also fear that telling parents or teachers about a bullying problem will actually make things worse. The school should generally be giving pupils the message that it's always right to tell if they are being bullied, or if they see someone else being bullied. It's important to notice any significant change in your child's behaviour or the mood, in case there is a problem and your child is just not telling anyone.

Most schools should recognise the vulnerability of a child with AS. It really helps if there is a particular person the aspie can go to if they are being bullied. At break times there should normally be some supervision of the school grounds by a members of staff who the aspie could go to if they were having problems. However, it's important that the aspie should not be put in a situation where the bully is called over and there is a three-way debate about whether the aspie was being bullied or not. This is likely to make the situation worse.

If some bullying does occur, try to get an accurate account of it. For example, note down when and where it happened, who was involved, who might have seen the bullying, what was said and what was done. The next step is to contact the school. Email works well as you can put in all the details of what happened and voice your concerns. If the incident is quite serious or quite urgent you may need to contact the school more quickly. The school will then decide what to do. Teachers will probably want to talk to the other people involved to get their side of the story, and then take it from there.

There will be a hierarchy of sanctions which can be applied to pupils who bully, depending on the severity of the issue. For example, a bully might get break time detentions, detention after school, isolation (which is when pupils are taken out of the class and have to work on their own for a period of time) or have privileges withdrawn, such as being banned from non-essential school trips for a period of time. For serious cases of physical assault, the head teacher could exclude a pupil.

It's also important for staff to work with the pupils doing the bullying so that they realise why what they did was wrong. It's possible for the teacher to talk to the person doing the bullying with the aim of getting them to realise that what they did is making the bullied child unhappy, and to talk about ways the situation could improve the situation. If there were any specific behaviours in the bullied child which aggravated the situation, such as repeatedly intruding on the other children's games, the teacher might also chat individually to the bullied child, to find ways of avoiding a similar situation. However, this in no way implies that it is the child's fault that he or she was bullied, and very often the bullied child has done nothing which might provoke a negative response.

The school's response to reports of bullying should be to take it seriously, to make it clear that the teachers do care, and to investigate thoroughly. It's important that teachers speak to any pupils involved individually, because otherwise the pupils will just back each other up with the same story. Talking individually is more likely to elicit the truth. As mentioned above, it would be quite unfair to round up the victim and bullies together in order to find out what happened. The victim is likely to be intimidated while the bullies will find reasons to justify their actions. Spoken to individually, they are all more likely to be responsive.

Teachers will monitor the situation to see if it recurs, and will be happy to receive feedback from parents on this issue. If the bullying continues and you are not confident that it is being dealt with effectively, you need to voice that concern to the teacher involved. If this doesn't help, the next step is to consult the head of year. If there is still no improvement, you may need to speak to the head teacher. It's important to be reasonable and to listen to what the staff say. At the same time, they should be willing to give your concerns careful consideration and to respond firmly to any incidents of bullying. Sometimes a half-hearted response from the school will actually make the situation worse because the bullies know they can get away with it. It's helpful to keep a written account of any bullying incidents that occur, as this will make the situation clear to all parties. If you have a discussion with the teacher, make a note of the main points afterwards, in order to be clear about what was said and what suggestions were made. Mostly schools do take the problem of bullying seriously, and everyone does their best to sort it out.

STRATEGIES TO HELP MAKE AN ASPIE LESS LIKELY TO BE BULLIED

There are things that can be done which may make people with AS less likely to be a target for bullies, and more able to deal with bullying when it does happen. With my suggestions I want to make it clear that I am not implying that it's the responsibility of the person with AS to change their behaviour if they want to avoid being bullied. No one deserves to be bullied, and people with AS should be proud of who they are. All schools should be working towards creating a safe and friendly environment where everyone can feel relaxed, accepted, and able to get on with the important business of learning. However, it's important to be realistic and to minimise the possibilities of being a target for bullying.

Assertiveness training can be very helpful for quiet children who are in danger of being picked on. The Kidscape website has a very good download available on assertiveness for children, and it's worth taking a look at this on its website (Kidscape 2010). Basic principles are that children need to be clear, direct and firm in their response to bullying. For example, if another boy is deliberately annoying you, say calmly, 'Stop doing that, I don't like it.' If he persists, either take yourself out of the situation or tell someone in authority. If a group of boys start calling you names as you walk past, try to seem calm and unconcerned and keep walking. Bullies like to provoke a reaction, for example by making you angry or a bit scared, so it's important to keep calm. That way they get bored and (let's hope) won't keep doing it. If someone deliberately comes up to you and is clearly trying to be nasty, for example by saying, 'Look, it's that idiot who can't kick a ball' (he'd probably put it more crudely), stay calm, act unconcerned and say something neutral like 'That's possibly true,' then walk away calmly. If you are in a situation you find threatening, such as being cornered by a group of boys, get out of there and find somewhere safe, where there are adults around. If someone asks you to do something you don't want to do, say 'No thanks.' If it's someone you regard as a friend, you can offer a different idea, such as, 'I don't want to lend you my book but you can have a look at it if you want.'

No one would claim that assertiveness entirely solves the problem, but it can enable an aspie to feel more confident and more in control. It really helps to practise role-playing the different situations, either in an assertiveness group or at home. That way the responses will come more easily when the aspie is in a difficult situation.

Bullies often pick on people who are different in some way, which includes those who have special needs. If an aspie has the help of a teaching assistant, it can help to be a bit discrete about this, so that he or she isn't marked out as being different from everybody else. Some aspies need one-to-one support, but often an assistant is shared by several pupils, in which case it's easier for the assistant to stay in the background. In primary school, children tend to accept that a classmate happens to have special help, so it's not such an issue. But in secondary school some kids have absolutely no scruples about who they bully and why.

Sometimes people with AS are encouraged to be completely up-front about this, so that it is made a subject for class discussion during a lesson. No one should be ashamed that they have AS. I firmly believe that society needs to become much more aware and accepting of Asperger syndrome. However, in secondary school it is quite likely that this will eventually result in teasing. Even if the people in the class respond with acceptance and respect, other pupils who get to hear of it will probably not behave so sensitively. I would admire any aspie who wanted to discuss Aspergers openly with the rest of the class, but I think it's important to understand the risk. In a primary school environment, particularly one in which pupils are encouraged to be open and supportive with one another, this is much less of an issue.

An alternative approach is to have a lesson about Asperger syndrome included in the general curriculum, for example in personal, social and health education (PSHE). That way pupils all learn about AS without the aspie having to make a personal disclosure. Personally, I feel strongly that autistic spectrum disorders should be taught as part of the national curriculum for PSHE, and so I would advise teachers to make time for it, and for parents to push for it.

Another factor that can result in someone with AS being bullied is behaving in a way that is obviously different. For example, some aspies have noticeable mannerisms, such as hand flapping or making random noises. It may be possible to work on these mannerisms in a one-to-one situation so that they are reduced. Obviously any work of this sort needs to be done sensitively and with an understanding of Asperger syndrome. Some guidance on how to do this is given in Chapter 4 of this book. However, aspies may actually have very little conscious control over these mannerisms, as they may do them almost without being aware of it when they get stressed or excited.

Some aspie behaviours tend to aggravate other kids and can make them a target for bullying. Extrovert aspies sometimes intrude on other children by trying to join in conversations and games when they are not welcome. They miss the social cues which would warn them to back off, and tend to be oblivious to hints. Other aspies might have a tendency to be a bit of a 'know-all' and to talk at great length about their favourite subjects. This can be annoying because it comes across as being patronising and it can also get quite boring. Again, it may be possible to work with the aspie and give them some guidelines about when it's okay to join in with other people, or how long to talk about their special interest. No one deserves to be bullied, however aggravating their behaviour is, but it is worth trying to reduce behaviours that may be considered annoying.

WHEN PEOPLE WITH AS BULLY

Occasionally one child with AS will develop a very controlling friendship with another child. Quite often the other child has AS but is a bit less able. The controlling child will tell the other child what to do, when to do it and how to do it. Sometimes both are happy with this arrangement. Friendships are often confusing because the people in it are not sure what the expectations are. It can be a relief to have expectations clearly laid out. So if an aspie often tells his friend to do things such as completing a particular level of a video game that evening and phoning afterwards to discuss it, this may not be a problem. It can become a problem if the friend gets stressed because he can't complete the level or if he hasn't really got time to do it because of homework. Often aspies don't know how to negotiate with their friends about what's a reasonable expectation and what isn't.

More worrying is the situation where an aspie starts to conduct a personal vendetta against another child, or even an adult. Some people with ASDs can be very unforgiving, because their thinking is quite black and white. If someone upsets them, in their mind, that person is a bad person. Jack still remembers minor incidents from childhood, when another child perhaps annoyed him. They still have the power to make him angry, and he will say things like, 'I hate that idiot!' It's possible that an aspie will decide a particular person is his enemy, and plot ways to deliberately annoy or upset this person. For example, it can be tempting to leave nasty messages on the other person's Facebook page. This kind of thing doesn't happen often but occasionally it can be a problem.

Sometimes an aspie can be involved in bullying because his 'friends' are persuading him to bully. They exploit his naivety and his keenness to have friends by getting him to carry out acts of bullying for which they don't want to get the blame. For example, they might persuade him to shout insults at the boy they are victimising, because they tell the aspie that this boy is a complete loser who deserves it. If the aspie does this and gets into trouble for it, they will deny any involvement.

Most commonly, there are times when an aspie can seem like the bully because he suddenly attacks another boy, perhaps in the middle of a lesson. What may have happened is that the other boy has been surreptitiously annoying him, perhaps prodding him or whispering 'freak' or 'loser', knowing that the aspie has a fierce temper. The other boy hopes to provoke an angry outburst that will disrupt the lesson and get the aspie into trouble. Bullies are very good at reading body language, and so know just how far to push someone, so they react just when the teacher is looking, and get their victim into trouble. This does not work on aspies. Remember, we are bad at reading body language, and at giving it off. Bullies may provoke and provoke and not seem to get a reaction, when in fact they are getting a very strong reaction. The pressure keeps building until suddenly the person with AS *appears* to go from 1 to 10, attacks the bully, and it is seen by the teachers as a complete over-reaction. The aspie is suspended for assault, and the bully gets off free. This is not right, and incidents like this need to be broken down. Yes, what they did was wrong, but their actions need to be considered in context, which is rarely done.

SUMMING UP

I realise that in focusing on the problem of bullying I may have given the impression that people with AS are bound to bullied, particularly at secondary school. Unfortunately, often people with AS are born targets, and are the most likely to be bulled. I'm hopeful that schools are changing their ethos, so that bullying is no longer accepted as an inevitable part of school life. However, it's a slow process.

If bullying does occur, the main principles seem to be as follows:

- Make a note of what happened in detail.

- Communicate your concerns to the school, giving accurate information.

- Make a note of any discussion you have with the teacher about what will be done.

- The situation needs to be monitored to see if the measures taken by the school have been effective.

- Any further incidents should be reported to the school.

- If you are not satisfied that the bullying is being dealt with effectively, speak to a senior member of staff, such as the head of year.

- If the problem still persists, if necessary speak to the head teacher, and if that doesn't help, write to the school governors.

In secondary school, particularly, it's useful to have a copy of the school's anti-bullying policy. This should lay out the procedures to be followed when dealing with bullying, and gives everyone guidance about what to do and what to expect. It's a useful document that you can refer to in communications with the school. Bullying is a difficult problem to deal with, and staff will normally do their best to sort it out.

When you are with your child:

- Encourage open communications.

- Explain that if other kids tell your child to keep something secret, it's sometimes for a bad reason, particularly at secondary school age.

- Define bullying.

- Let your child know that it's important to tell someone if they think they are being bullied.

- If your child is being bullied they need to know something will be done about this, and that whatever is done will not make things worse.

- People will persist in trying to sort out the problem.

- Your child has a right to be educated without being harassed, intimidated or persecuted by other pupils.

- No one deserves to be bullied and being bullied is not a sign that your child is somehow not good enough as a person. Bullies just get a kick out of bullying and will bully for no good reason at all.

Although making anti-bullying policies mandatory for all schools was a big step forward, it's important to remember that the anti-bullying policy of any school is effective only if staff are encouraged to implement it, and supported when they do. Pupils need to be regularly reminded of the anti-bullying ethos of the school, and encouraged to tell staff if they are being bullied or if they see someone else being bullied. Teachers need to take reports of bullying seriously and take action, making sure they monitor the situation afterwards to make sure it doesn't start up again. Often a half-hearted response makes things worse. Most teachers do understand the misery that bullying can cause and will do their best to sort things out.

Parents and teachers need to keep reminding policy makers that bullying is still a huge issue in schools, so that it stays on the agenda. There is a danger that in hard times the policy makers only focus on the educational aspects of school and overlook bullying, thinking they've dealt with it by insisting every school has an anti-bullying policy. In reality bullying is an education issue because children who are bullied often achieve much poorer results than could be expected from their general level of ability. We also need to highlight the fact that people with AS are often more vulnerable to bullying, and need support. Lots of aspies are talented, and most are conscientious and hard working. It would be a great loss to the country's workforce if their education was derailed because of bullying.

9

TOOLBOX

Popular Problems and Helpful Hints

Please note that I am not qualified to give medical advice. You should always consult a qualified practitioner before undertaking any therapy or treatment.

In your knowledge and experience, is a GF/CF diet helpful? Should I try this with my child?

Some people swear by gluten-free (GF) and casein-free (CF) diets, saying that they see great improvements in children on the spectrum, while others have tried these diets and found that they see no changes whatsoever. Some people have even made claims that 'all traces' of autism or Asperger syndrome have left their child. I have certainly met people on the diet who say that it has helped. But equally I know some for whom it has had no effect. Research Autism (2011) has not found any conclusive evidence for CF/GF diets, but says that more research is needed. There is also some anecdotal evidence that people on the spectrum can suffer from gastro-intestinal problems.

Thus far I have not heard of any major health problems with going on the diet, although some parents have reported odd behaviour as a result, for example 'smelling' out gluten in various odd items – like wallpaper paste and thus eating wallpaper. However, this seems to be limited to the very autistic end of the spectrum. It may be that your child will find this diet helpful, and I would never advise against trying it. I would, however, advise you to look at some books on this, for example Luke Jackson's *A User Guide to the GF/CF Diet* to see what is involved (Jackson 2002a), and then consult your GP or a dietician before embarking on the diet.

Will my child with Asperger syndrome be better in a mainstream state school or a special school?

This is a question to which there is no right answer. Everyone is different, and so different situations will suit different people. I know people on the spectrum who have done well unsupported in a mainstream school. Often the school has agreed to make adaptations, and takes a strong interest in supporting the child wherever it is needed. It certainly has the advantages of being free and providing a 'normal' education. However, there are also a lot of horror stories, of which I am one. Sometimes a unit attached to a mainstream school can be the answer – the dedicated support in a mainstream environment is often successful. Certainly my youngest brother has found this to be ideal at primary school, because he is very social.

Mainstream private schools I know can work well. Since parents are paying them, management are probably more enthusiastic to help with problems. I know a few people who have gone to private schools and remained undiagnosed because the support they got was what they needed, and the environment seemed to suit them. Indeed, often the private school emphasis on hard work and academia pays off for academic aspies: in mainstream school there is a much stronger emphasis on fitting in.

Specialist private schools for autism and Asperger syndrome are often good. The support given is usually very specific and tailored to the child or young person. However, it is often much harder to get funding for places at these schools as they are often very expensive. They are often so far away that students have to board, which may not be suitable for your child.

The fact is, the right environment and the right support is what is needed – I found it at a specialist private school, others have found it at mainstream private schools, and many have done so at mainstream public schools. I advise you to look at all your options carefully, with your child, and see if you can find somewhere that 'feels' right.

Did drugs help you deal with your Aspergers and depression?

I was eventually put on 20mg of fluoxetine (Prozac) for my depression, after trying many other antidepressants. I was on that for four years and experienced minimal side effects. I am currently on melatonin (3mg) to help with sleep. Melatonin is currently out of favour because studies have shown that it has no effect on most people. But I have found it works for me. My problems with sleep were not caused by my Aspergers but by my environment. With my Aspergers came an inability to 'switch off' at night, and mild hypersensitivity to noise. This meant that when I was trying to get to sleep, everything would seem really loud and I couldn't stop thinking. *Drugs should not be taken to 'deal with' Asperger syndrome*, as Asperger syndrome is not something that needs treating. Drugs can be useful when the environment and the Asperger syndrome clash – for example my depression. I don't think drugs should be a long-term solution in most cases, rather a short-term stop gap, enabling the individual to get though a bad time, or to have psychological therapies that will eventually eliminate the need for the enabling drug. Sometimes this isn't the case, for example with my sleep, but I think it is something that should be the goal, at least at the start.

How can I get a diagnosis for my child?

In the UK, the standard route to diagnosis is to make an appointment with your GP, and ask for a referral to a specialist (usually a psychiatrist or paediatrician), who will then make a formal diagnosis. While this works in theory, waiting lists are often long, and sometimes people need to try other routes to getting a diagnosis. Alternatively, you can make an appointment with a private psychiatrist or paediatrician who can also make a diagnosis. The NAS Helpline and website has some great advice about practitioners and how to get a diagnosis (see www.autism.org. uk/about-autism/all-about-diagnosis.aspx). Outside of the UK, the route to diagnosis will be different, but the main concern is to ensure that the clinician giving the diagnosis is suitably qualified.

I suspect my adult sibling may have Asperger syndrome – what can I do?

In these situations, I tend to think that it is usually best to explain to them your concerns. It may well be they are having problems that they are keeping from everyone else, and that a diagnosis, or even just reading a bit about Asperger syndrome could answer a lot of questions for them. It is very important that they are told in the right way. Often people are told of their diagnosis and it comes off as being a very negative thing, which sets the tone for how they see it for a long time. The fact is that Asperger syndrome can be a positive thing, and so putting it across in a positive way is key. The way in which you can tell him is rather varied. Some people drop subtle hints, or recommend they read an interesting book on Asperger syndrome and see if they twig that they have Asperger syndrome. Others try a more direct approach and ask 'Do you think you have this thing called Asperger syndrome?' and present them with some reading material on it. It may be that they don't think they do have it, and they may not. It may be that they have it to a small extent, but not enough to cause problems or warrant a diagnosis.

Having said all that, there are adults I know who certainly have Asperger syndrome, but who don't need and don't want a diagnosis as they get on fine. It may be that telling them would have no effect, or in a small minority of cases cause them problems. This is again an instance where you should 'go with your gut' as to whether to tell them or not. But if you do decide to tell them, then I recommend the ways outlined above. Above all, keep it positive and don't just leave them once you have talked to them. They may well need some support from you afterwards.

Is getting a proper diagnosis important? Why?

Getting a proper diagnosis is important, because the impact it can have is huge. It can mean that schools take more notice, that council and social services, opportunities for specialist education, and other government-centred help and care suddenly become available (albeit after some paperwork!). A diagnosis from a qualified practitioner is a key that will open doors for you. After getting a diagnosis of Asperger syndrome, my school took a bit more notice of my problems, and it enabled me to access other services that could support me.

My child doesn't want to mix with other children – what should I do?

Aspies are like mules in some ways: when we want to do something and someone is telling us to do the other we will often dig our heels in and not budge. Unfortunately, if a person decides they don't want to mix with other children, sometimes there isn't much you can do. It is impossible to force someone to socialise. You could lock them in a vault with someone and wait, but unless they want to, they will do little more than acknowledge their presence. However, humans are by nature social creatures, and that human instinct to socialise is still there in Asperger syndrome. I remember spending eight months or so hardly ever leaving the house (for maybe three hours per week max), and by the end of it I felt starved and desperate to socialise. The problem is we don't know how to socialise; it is something scary for us, and hard to work out. What I generally recommend in these situations is to ask about their day at school – specifically if they played with anyone, talked to anyone, generally gently encouraging them, and helping where needed (but not forcing the issue). Secondary socialisation is the key in this situation. Teachers can try to involve the children in games and other activities where socialisation is a by-product. For example, playing a game in teams involves socialisation, but it is a by-product of the primary activity. Equally, at work, the primary goal is (usually) to produce something, to manage someone, generally to be productive, but socialisation is necessary to achieve this goal, and social skills are improved through it – that same practice is what we are trying to do here.

Do you think that encouraging my child to do out-of-school activities such as horse riding or football is a good idea?

Getting an aspie child out and about can be hard, and so I definitely think that trying to nurture any interests in out-of-school activities is a good thing. Often when school is the only source thing they do outside, it leads to them being confined to home a lot. I think things like horse riding – something noncompetitive and involving animals – are good. While we can be good at competitive sports, we can sometimes get too competitive. We don't just *like* to win – we *need* to win! And so trying something noncompetitive may be good. Equally animals are often good (unless the child has a fear of them), as they are often a great source of comfort.

My son with Aspergers is eight years but is still not toilet trained. Should I force the issue or keep him in nappies until he is ready? Do you have any tips?

The first think to keep in mind is that there could be a sensory issue here. We feel a full bladder or bowls through sensory input – and if that sensory input is not getting through then that could be the cause of the toilet training problems. It might be worth seeking out an expert in sensory issues. If it is simply that he doesn't want to be toilet trained, or sees no need for it, then you could try some reward strategies. Things like building up points for a clean nappy in the morning/afternoon/evening, and after getting say 30 points, getting something he wants. If he attends a specialist school, they may be willing to help too. People with Aspergers are often sensitive to 'being normal', they often want to be normal, and so trying to use that as motivation can also work well. Children with Asperger syndrome should eventually become toilet trained (albeit late in some cases). I would recommend you keep trying. When it does finally start to 'click', it helps if there is help at hand.

My brother with Aspergers still lives with my aged parents. While he is a useful person to have around them at this time, I worry about how he will be able to cope when they are no longer around. What can I do?

In the UK I would recommend that you consider suggesting to your parents to ask social services for a social care assessment. There are schemes like supported living where individuals can have a lot of independence, and just have support workers come in every now and then to help with bills, budgeting, cooking, work etc. This sounds like the sort of level of support your brother may need. It may well be that in time he becomes more independent, and is able to live unsupported. The NAS Helpline can also offer advice on this issue.

What's your view on ABA, Son-Rise and other intensive early intervention programmes?

First of all I would recommend that you have a look at the Research Autism website at www.researchautism.net. Some of these therapies have so far failed to have been validated by independent research. That doesn't necessarily mean that they don't work, but you should be aware of the latest research before committing time and money into these therapies.

While some therapies have been shown to be effective in some cases, in many more cases there has been little or no effect. Like the GF/CF diet question earlier, this is very much a hit and miss area. Some therapies can be very expensive. I do think that early interventions can make a big difference. However, these early interventions are not like ABA (Applied Behavioural Analysis) or Son-Rise, but rather early diagnosis, early identification of problems, and tackling them on a one-to-one basis that is tailor-made for the individual.

It is important to talk to a qualified professional who is independent from the programme for advice before embarking on any intervention or therapy – some therapies have been found to do more harm than good. I would also emphasise the need to define a base level, to compare with later on to see if there has been any improvement.

My 14-year-old son with Asperger syndrome has been excluded from school for hitting another child. The school say they don't know why he lashed out, but he's never violent at home. What should I do?

My first thoughts are that he could be being bullied and so could be retaliating. Or he could be retaliating against someone completely innocent who just happened to be around to act as an outlet for his anger. Another possibility is that another child did something that has been wrongly perceived as bullying by your son. With all of these options, it is really important to ask all parties to explain exactly what happened – you may then be able to piece together the sequence of events and whether there were any misunderstandings.

Another option is a sensory one. It may be that something sensory happened that triggered this. For example, hypersensitivity to sound could trigger aggression if, for example, a school bell has just gone off causing a big fight or flight response; added to stress, it could cause aggression. Hypersensitivity to touch is another common one – lots of people trying to get to lessons quickly in narrow corridors. Try asking him if anything was annoying him or causing him stress, which may give you a clue as to why he lashed out. In any case, good communication with the school to resolve the problem and make sure it doesn't happen again should be a key objective.

My son is a very fussy eater. He's underweight, but not dangerously so. Should I be worried?

Fussy eating is a relatively common problem with children with Asperger syndrome. If it becomes a serious problem, you should consult a doctor or dietician. Sometimes, it can resolve itself. As a child I was always rather picky about what I chose to eat. Often it is something that goes away over time. What made me eat was social pressure – not wanting to stand out as someone who was really fussy. Also when I was on holiday I had a more limited choice and had to eat different foods. Eventually I saw that I cannot be a kid about it any more and that to get where I need in life, I needed to be more flexible with my eating habits. So no, I wouldn't be too worried. It is certainly something to keep an eye on, and it is always worth trying to get children to try new foods, but this usually resolves itself by the mid-teens. Other things you can do to help encourage them is getting them to cook the food themselves – sometimes taking pride in what they have cooked, or seeing what is in their food or how it is made can help. Equally hunger will often play a big part – it is always best to try new foods out when they are hungry!

**My eight-year-old son with Aspergers runs out of the house
if he loses his temper. He has no road sense, and we live
one block away from a busy road. What can I do?**

There are likely to be two possible reasons for him doing this.
First, he may do it as he knows it is something you don't like, and
so he is letting you know how angry he is. Second, it could be that
he needs some space to calm down and he feels he can get this by
going outside or running. The obvious thing is to try and get him
to run outside or to simply leave him alone in the room for a while.
You could putting an extra lock on the door high up (and out of
reach to anyone but adults). This should make it harder for him
to get out. It may be necessary to extend the locks to windows.
However, this does not solve the underlying problem, which needs
to be addressed.

For a more permanent solution, you could try making an angry
area. For example, a garden shed or summer house – where only
he is allowed. Another quiet place used in our house is the car: it
is quiet, secure and comfy, so they can just relax. If it is that they
need to let the anger out physically, something like swing ball or
a punch bag can often be useful. Let's hope that in time he will
develop some road sense, and so this problem will no longer be
an issue.

**I'm running out of patience with dealing with my two
Aspergers sons and one daughter. I am a single mum and
don't have any support. I'm worried if I call social services
my children will be taken into care. What should I do?**

While social services can take children into care, it is always as a
last resort. Their priority is to keep families together, not to split
them up, and so they will often provide a significant amount of
help in the home to support parents. Many councils have a care
scheme, whereby trained carers come into your home and help
out – either cooking for the kids, taking them out; some even
arrange long 48-hour breaks so you can have a mini-holiday. I
would strongly advise looking into this by ringing up your local
social services office and asking for an assessment.

There are also various play schemes that are Aspergers-specific or for disabilities. They can also help provide a break, although there is often a cost involved in these. If you live in the UK then I would also recommend you contact the NAS Helpline, as they have a lot of information about services in your area and can advise you further.

My son has failed to get a place in the special school I wanted, because there are no spaces available. I don't think there are any other local schools that would take him. The local education authority is suggesting a residential placement at a special school specifically for ASD students. But I'm not sure he's old enough to cope. He's ten years old.

It is by no means impossible for a ten-year-old child with Aspergers to live away from home. Young people with Aspergers can be very resilient and can cope with a lot. Providing he can get over the initial stress that the move to boarding school would entail, he could do well in school. The residential school will have lots of experience in getting children and young people through the stress of moving. They may be able to suggest ways to help ease the transition – like doing a few day-long sessions, and building up to overnight – that is what a lot of places do. I moved to residential college when I was 17 and for the first term I was struggling to cope. But after that it became a lot easier and in the end the college turned out to be the best move I ever made, as I finally had the support I needed.

Overall, it really depends on the child. If this is the only option available, it is worth trying. I would advise you to liaise with the school to make it as easy as possible for your son. It helps if there are opportunities to come home at weekends.

My son has ADHD (Attention Deficit Hyperactivity Disorder) as well as Asperger syndrome. The child psychiatrist is suggesting Ritalin, but I have heard some very bad things about this drug. What's your opinion?

Ritalin is certainly an option. It is widely used in the United States. Unfortunately, in some areas, there seems to be a culture whereby Ritalin is seen as a 'treatment' for AS and that whenever someone has problems, they are dosed up to make the lives of people around them easier. Particularly in high doses, people on the spectrum have reported that it makes them feel cloudy, and that they don't feel like themselves. In low doses, it seems to have a more calming effect than a 'doping' effect. It may be helpful on a short- to medium-term basis if it is used alongside other interventions like therapy from a psychologist. I personally would be wary about using it as a long-term solution, particularly in high doses. However, I must stress that I am not a doctor. Your child's psychiatrist, on the other hand, is. He or she should listen to your concerns, and try to address them before writing the prescription. Ultimately, I would never advise you to go against medical advice.

My son with Aspergers likes computer games. He's ten years old and spends hours at a time on these games. Is it a good idea to let him spend this amount of time playing games? Are there any games you can recommend?

It is very common for people on the spectrum to get really into computer games. Whereas neurotypicals may enjoy them, they often space them out with socialisation. On the other hand, people with Aspergers may not socialise as much, and will therefore spend more time playing computer games. This in itself is not a bad thing, but when it becomes all that they do, then it is probably worth looking at trying to get them interested in other things. Whether it is serious enough to warrant your intervention is really a judgement call on your behalf. But if you decide to try and wean him off computer games a bit, then there are things you can do to help. Some PC software allows times to be controlled when the computer can be used. This can be very handy as they are regular and not swayed by arguments! If he plays it in the evening, that is often the easiest time to tackle it – try and end it a bit earlier (starting, say, only ten minutes early, and then increasing to cut down the time). This also helps with sleep. I would not recommend cutting it out directly after school or after homework – they are very useful then as a bit of escapism – and sometimes we do need that. It is also worth getting timers (you can get some in traffic light form), which act as a good visual cue to how long is left, and often result in fewer tantrums at the end.

I'm considering home educating my five-year-old aspie son because I don't think he's ready for school. Am I allowed to do this? How will I know when he's ready for school? He doesn't have a statement, but I wouldn't be looking to get additional support from the education authority.

In the UK you are allowed to home school your child. But you should seek advice from organisations such as Education Otherwise (www.education-otherwise.net) who can provide guidance on this. Home schooling can work well for children with Asperger syndrome. They are in a safe environment that they know. However, I would probably discourage it beyond the age of ten years. The trouble is, for GCSEs, which all employers look for, children really need a secondary school environment. They will need teachers who are familiar with the subject. For example, for a GCSE English paper, while you can read examiners' reports, and see what they look for, you still won't have the experience needed. Equally for science subjects – it is almost impossible to do any experiments which really aid understanding. Because of this, I really think that for *most* people, being taught by teachers is best. In the UK, to stand the best chance at secondary school, they will ideally need to attend a primary school for at least a year or so to get used to a classroom environment, and to the different style of work. They will also be able to sit the Year 6 SATs exam – while this doesn't give them any qualifications, it does help the school assess aptitude in subjects.

Home tuition is also often a big strain on parents – earning money, keeping the household, and teaching is no easy task. However, if you feel you want to do it and think it is the best option, then go for it. It is certainly less stressful for the child, and exam free. There are home schooling groups that meet up so the children have some time to socialise with others their age too – as well as provide support for parents. The socialisation element is particularly important – even if we don't like it, that bit of social interaction, or watching social interaction, can be important

There are also some home study programmes that might be appropriate. I used Satellite Virtual Schools for about a year when I could no longer cope in secondary school. This gets round the problems of experience and equipment for teaching at home.

As for knowing when he will be ready for school – I am not sure there is ever a right time. For any child it is a big step, more so for aspies. However, I think that for most families it is a step that needs to be taken and I do believe that in most cases, sooner is better than later.

I am considering sending my ten-year-old son with Aspergers to a private school when he comes to the end of his stay at the local state primary school. I like the idea of small classes and can afford to pay the fees if I go back to work. Do you have any advice?

Private schools can certainly be very successful for many aspies, and if you can afford them I would certainly recommend looking at them. But you need to be sure that the support that your son needs will be provided. The only thing to consider is that, like neurotypicals, not all aspies are academic. It may be that he shows an aptitude for academia, in which case it is likely to be a good choice. However if he is bright, but not academic, then maybe finding a good mainstream state school might be as good an option.

My Aspergers son, aged 12, is very disorganised at school and at home. Do you know of any strategies or aids that may help?

I think generally with teenagers there is usually a bit more disorganisation than usual, but it is often more pronounced with teenagers on the spectrum. Personally, what I found really useful was a PDA (personal digital computer or palmtop). I found it a lot more effective than a school diary as I could not read my writing, so when I made notes of homework or of things to do, I couldn't read them! Could this be the case for your son?

To help organise things for school, it may be helpful to come up with a list of what needs to be packed in the school bag every night and simply getting in the habit of doing it every evening, say, before tea. For homework, I found for me the best thing was to simply do them on the day they are set. It is much easier to get into the habit of thinking back over each lesson of the day and thinking if they set any homework and then doing it, than just occasionally wondering if any homework was set and then having to do it for several days!

I would worry less about untidiness at home, as there is only so much influence parents have. I would first concentrate on school, and let home be an easy and safe place. Maybe over time the same good habits will transfer to home – but it really is all about getting into good habits, which will require a lot of nagging!

My son aged nine has developed some facial tics and some repetitive behaviour. I wonder if this is due to stress at school? The school is aware of his diagnosis, but he is not statemented and receives little support at school.

Often repetitive behaviour is very soothing for us (see Chapter 4 on stimming, obsessions and rituals). It may be that the repetitive behaviour is simply a way your child has found of making school more fun or interesting. They can also be ways of relieving stress. We all have things we do when we are stressed – chew gum, pace, etc. – most people have some little behaviour they exhibit when they are stressed and our rituals are very much like that.

Tics can be a sign of stress, and sometimes repetitive behaviour can be a way to relieve stress, so it could be that he is getting rather stressed. It may be worth asking questions to see if there is anything that could be bothering him at school (for example, was there any bit of school he didn't like? Was there anything which was hard or frustrating?). If there are things that consistently cause him stress, then talking to the school and asking if something could be done to help elevate this stress.

Tics can be caused by things other than stress, so if there is no obvious cause then I would recommend seeing a doctor.

My 12-year-old son is very depressed. He won't talk to me about it, but he is spending more and more time in his room and is becoming bad tempered. Is this normal teenage behaviour or should I be worried?

To an extent, it is likely to be normal teenage behaviour. Wanting more privacy, being more stressed, and indeed more depressed is just a part of growing up nowadays. Having said that, an alarmingly high number of students (not just aspies) at secondary school have either contemplated or tried suicide. Unfortunately this statistic is even higher for people with Asperger syndrome, and so being alert and trying to prevent it starting is key.

I would recommend you keep trying to talk to him, and he may let something slip out. The hard thing is finding a way into him. It is also worth asking teachers how he seems at school, and whether he seems unhappy. There are other signs of depression to look out for, for example a marked increase or decrease in appetite, insomnia, or a loss of interest in hobbies or activities he has previously enjoyed. Keeping an eye out for these is very important. If you suspect he may be depressed, then there are various things to watch out for and I have covered these elsewhere in this book. If the school has a counselling service, it may be worth asking the counsellor to talk to him to see how he is. This could be done as a 'spot check' or that one of the teachers was worried about them. This approach may be advisable as most aspies are likely to be very resentful if they learn that you are 'meddling' in their school life. If you are really worried, I would always recommend talking to a doctor or psychologist.

My father-in-law recently died, and although we are coping as a family, my son keeps reminding my mother-in-law that Granddad is dead. My mother-in-law isn't very understanding and naturally gets upset. But my aspie son doesn't know why. Do you have any ideas on how to deal with this?

The problem here may be that he is surprised that nobody is talking about it. It is a major change, one he is not used to, and yet nobody is talking about it. I would recommend you try sitting him down and talking to him about it. Try to answer any questions he may have. If that does not work, then try to explain that Grandma really misses Granddad and that it would be really helpful if he did not remind her. Failing that then simply having an 'inappropriate topics for conversation' list, and putting Granddad's death on it, may be useful. I know several individuals who do not know what is appropriate conversation and keep a list of topics which they shouldn't talk about to people apart from parents.

My son has a phobia about small dogs and it means we cannot take him out walking or visit friends with dogs. What can I do?
Phobias that start to take over people's lives is an area that psychologists are trained to deal with. If a neurotypical had the same phobia, and it was impacting a great deal on their life, then they would get a referral from their doctor. There is no reason the same cannot apply to someone on the spectrum. If you want to try some things at home, then trying gradual desensitisation may help. For example, if you have a friend with a small docile dog, ask them to come on over with the dog and stay a door away (preferably behind a glass door). Let's hope that after a while (maybe several hours) he may feel safe around that dog at that distance and with a door. Then perhaps moving to having the dog on a leash tethered somewhere outdoors at the same sort of distance with the door open. Then when they are happy with that, being outside with the dog tethered and so on. The gradual desensitisation process can take a very long time, and if it causes a really high amount of distress for your son, then I would definitely leave it to a trained psychologist.

When should I tell my son that he has Asperger syndrome? What is the best approach?
I get asked this question a lot. The truth of the matter is that everyone is so different that it is impossible to give a time. While telling a child early in life tends to eliminate the shock factor, parents are a far better judge and if they feel a certain time is inappropriate, then I would always recommend going with that decision.

As for the best approach, it needs to be positive. The child needs to see Asperger syndrome as something that, yes, can cause problems, but is also something good. Depending on age, giving them a book on Asperger syndrome can be good. For 12+, Luke Jackson's (2002b) book *Freaks, Geeks and Asperger Syndrome* is good. For younger kids, I think that *All Cats have Asperger Syndrome* (Hoopmann 2006) is a very good way of introducing it.

Pointing out people who have Asperger syndrome and who are successful or historical figures thought to have Asperger syndrome can be really helpful. I'd recommend getting out from your library the book *The Genesis of Artistic Creativity: Asperger's Syndrome and the Arts* by Michael Fitzgerald (2005). This book highlights several historical figures who may have had Asperger syndrome.

AFTERWORD

I started writing this book way back when I was a fresher at St Andrews. The idea was essentially to condense several of my talks into one book: designed for parents, and teachers, of children and young adults at the high functioning end of the spectrum. In particular, I wanted to focus on practical solutions, rather than giving parents with a freshly diagnosed child a book on theory.

This was a challenge to write. While I can happily sit down and write about a topic, I have always been a perfectionist. As soon as I think of a new problem, a new solution, or a new way of thinking about it, I want to put it in. However, we are finally there. It has taken me many hours of writing, but it has also taken my mum, Julia, many hours of editing, for which I am very grateful. I have learned many lessons on how to write in doing this, and I hope my next book will take a little less time and require a lot less editing. However, I am indebted to Mum for taking my ramblings and making them easy to read. I am also very grateful to Jessica Kingsley for her unending patience in allowing me and Mum to do this and get it right.

I hope what you take away from this is an understanding and appreciation for what it is like to be on the spectrum, and the difficulties we face. Most importantly, I hope you take away hope. By its nature, this book has been negative at times: addressing problems, rather than spending a long time talking about strengths. But we do have strengths – whether it be our specialist subjects, our logical and systemising ability, or even the ability to make someone smile. Nobody on the spectrum should be ashamed or held back by their diagnosis – everybody can contribute in some way to society.

All it takes is a little bit of the right support.

REFERENCES

APA (American Psychiatric Association) (2000) *Diagnostic and Statistical Manual of Mental Disorders* (DSM-IV-TR). Washington, DC: APA.

Attwood, T. (1998) *Asperger's Syndrome: A Guide for Parents and Professionals.* London: Jessica Kingsley Publishers.

Attwood, T. (2001) 'Understanding the Autistic Spectrum.' Lecture given at the NAS Surrey branch Conference.

Baron-Cohen, S. (1999) 'The Extreme-male-brain Theory of Autism.' In H. Tager-Flusberg (ed.) *Neurodevelopmental Disorders.* Cambridge, MA: The MIT Press.

Baron-Cohen, S. (2002) 'Is Asperger's Syndrome Necessarily a Disability?' Available at www.autismresearchcentre.com/docs/papers/2002_BC_ASDisability.pdf, accessed on 27 July 2011.

Baron-Cohen, S. (2008) 'Theories of the autistic mind.' *The Psychologist 21,* 2, 112–116.

Beck, A.T., Rush, A.J., Shaw, B.F. and Emery, G. (1979) *Cognitive Therapy of Depression.* New York: Guilford Press.

Fitzgerald, M. (2005) *The Genesis of Artistic Creativity: Asperger's Syndrome and the Arts.* London: Jessica Kingsley Publishers.

Frith, U. (2003) *Autism: Explaining the Enigma.* Malden, MA: Blackwell.

Hoopmann, K. (2006) *All Cats have Asperger Syndrome.* London: Jessica Kingsley Publishers.

Jackson, L. (2002a) *A User Guide to the GF/CF Diet for Autism, Asperger Syndrome and AD/HD.* London: Jessica Kingsley Publishers.

Jackson, L. (2002b) *Freaks, Geeks and Asperger Syndrome: A User Guide to Adolescence.* London: Jessica Kingsley Publishers.

Kidscape (2005) 'Anti-Bullying Policy for Schools.' Available at www.kidscape.org.uk/assets/downloads/Antibullypolicy.rtf, accessed on 4 August 2011.

Kidscape (2010) 'Assertiveness for Children.' Available at www.kidscape.org.uk/assets/downloads/assertivenessforchildren.pdf, accessed on 4 August 2011.

Mehrabian, A. (1981) *Silent Messages: Implicit Communication of Emotions and Attitudes,* 2nd edn. Belmont, CA: Wadsworth.

NAS (National Autistic Society) (2010) *B is for Bullied: The Experiences of Children with Autism and their Families.* London: NAS. Available at www.autism.org.uk/bullyingengland, accessed on 27 July 2011.

Research Autism (2011) 'Gluten-Free, Casein-Free Diet and Autism.' Available at www.researchautism.net/interventionitem.ikml?ra=1, accessed on 29 July 2011.

Seligman, M.E.P. (1992) *Helplessness: On Depression, Development, and Death.* San Francisco, CA: W.H. Freeman.

Wing, L. (1981) *Asperger Syndrome: A Clinical Account.* London: National Autistic Society.

Wing, L. and Gould, J. (1979) 'Severe impairments of social interaction and associated abnormalities in children: Epidemiology and classification.' *Journal of Autism and Developmental Disorders 9*, 1, 11–29.

WHO (World Health Organization) (1992) *International Statistical Classification of Diseases and Related Health Problems* (ICD-10). Geneva: WHO.

INDEX